Reimagining Discipleship

Living Well
When Jesus is King

DEDICATION

To my family and friends – partners in serving Jesus our King:
May our lives and friendships be worth remembering and celebrating
even after we step fully into Jesus' coming reign over all creation. Life has
been quite the adventure, and I'm so thankful to be sharing it with you!

And to Jody, Seth, Matt, and Sam:
You guys are the best! I'm so thankful to share this life with you and that
we can look forward to an eternity together serving in God's kingdom.
Thank you so much for every late night, early morning, and weekend that
you gave up for me to see this project through. I love you so much. You
have been my motivation throughout this whole process. May you each
continue growing as disciples of Jesus Christ. May you love well. May you
be a blessing everywhere you go. May you know the Lord more and more.
And may your life always be shaped by the anticipation of Jesus' return
and his coming reign!

CONTENTS

SERIES PREFACE: FIRST THINGS FIRST

When Jesus is King   2
Repentance & Transformation   4
Expectations & Commitment   9

PART 1: WHAT'S THE STORY

Introduction   12
Week 1: Parameters   14
Week 2: Flow   19
Week 3: Perspective   26
Week 4: Inevitability   34

PART 2: WHO IS JESUS?

Introduction   42
Week 5: The Son of Man   44
Week 6: The Son of David   52
Week 7: The Son of God   59
Week 8: The Messiah   65

PART 3: WHAT IS THE CHURCH?

Introduction   72
Week 9: A Storied Church   74
Week 10: The GREAT Church   79
Week 11: The Body of Christ   87
Week 12: Heirs   93

PART 4: WHAT NOW?

Introduction   100
Week 13: Resurrection Life   101
Week 14: Born Again   107
Week 15: Eternal Life   113
Week 16: Temples   118

Epilogue   124

APPENDIX

Old Testament Readings   126
Leader's Guidelines   127
The Good News...in 100 Seconds   130
A Word from the Author   132

Living Well WJK Series Preface:
FIRST THINGS FIRST

WHEN JESUS IS KING

Luke 19

Take a moment to read Luke 19:11-27. In this chapter, Jesus and the disciples are heading to Jerusalem. As they approach Israel's capital, the disciples assume that the kingdom Jesus had been announcing for three years is finally going to appear. Aware of their misguided assumption, Jesus stops to tell the disciples a story – a story about a man who would be king, an unexpected delay in his coming, and an ensuing dilemma for those left to determine their fates during his absence.

Our journey together begins with this parable because Jesus' words are as relevant for us today as they were to his first disciples. While the delay in the King's return is no longer a surprise, we're still living amidst the same dilemma as we wait: the world is hostile toward any would-be king claiming authority over them. And here, amidst the anticipation and the hostility, we come to the main point of Jesus' parable:

The lives we live as we await the King's return will determine our places in his eternal kingdom.

This parable is not just relevant for Christians. Every person you or I will ever know is living out their lives between verses 14 & 15. Jesus has claimed to be the King, and the world is waiting to see what the outcome will be. This means that Luke 19 is not just some religious story. It's the human story. And in this story, people emerge with one of three stereotypical responses:

1. **Independence/Rebellion:** These "citizens" are insulted at the King's claim of authority over their lives and blatantly oppose his reign.

2. **Cautious Neutrality:** These "servants" of the King lack confidence in his return and in the reality of his coming kingdom. Rather than risk association with the King amidst a hostile environment, they opt for cautious neutrality as they await the outcome. They don't blatantly oppose the King, but neither are they willing to invest their lives in the King's business. Instead, they pursue their own agendas as they wait to see what becomes of the kingdom.

3. **Faithful/Allegiant Service:** Faithful servants of the King put their lives and personal agendas on the line to dedicate themselves to the King's business during his absence. They live in confident anticipation of the King's return and his subsequent reign.

LIVING WELL WHEN JESUS IS KING takes Jesus' words seriously. It's goal & purpose is for us to learn to live more and more as faithful servants. It's grounded on the faith that we're already living when Jesus is King and that our lives here & now are of eternal significance. It's written in anticipation of the day that we'll stand before Jesus Christ and hear the words:

"Well done, good and faithful servant. Because you have been faithful in a little, you shall have authority in my kingdom." (Luke 19:17)

John 15

For further clarity, let's turn to John 15. In this passage, Jesus offers another snapshot of the life he envisions for us as we await his return. (Read John 15:1-17.)

As he did in Luke 19 & throughout his ministry, Jesus once again insists that the way we live matters greatly. Whether it's doing "the king's business" or "bearing fruit", God's intention for each of us is to impact the lives of those around us (15:2). This is not a high calling for a select few. This is God's purpose for all followers of Jesus Christ.

From his perspective, it's the impact of our lives (not our beliefs or affections) by which we set ourselves apart as disciples of Jesus Christ (15:8).

In John 15, Jesus adds another critical element to remember as we move forward:

Living well when Jesus is King is not something we accomplish in our own strength and wisdom.

We only "bear fruit" to the degree we learn to ABIDE IN JESUS CHRIST. Then, like branches of a vine, WE DO WHAT COMES NATURALLY. We bear fruit.

So living well when Jesus is King is not just about meeting our quota of good deeds. It's about living a different kind of life in which Jesus has become our source & identity. The impact of our lives is then natural to the kind of people we have become.

The journey ahead...
This is our pursuit in the journey before us: to serve our King faithfully. To learn a way of life in which we're abiding in Jesus Christ at every moment. We're going to work hard to see things the way Jesus did. To sacrifice for something greater than ourselves. To learn to live for his purposes. And along the way, we'll become the kind of people for whom this all comes more and more naturally.

We are taking this intentional journey together because such a life requires intentionality. Living well when Jesus is King means living outside the status quo. It means learning to live differently. It means learning to think differently. It means embracing Jesus as our King here & now so that when he returns, we'll find ourselves quite at home as we transition into his eternal kingdom.

REPENTANCE & TRANSFORMATION

"WHEN JESUS IS KING" (the previous section) constitutes the "What" of this series. It's the overarching vision, purpose & goal. We ended with a thought on intentionality – because living well when Jesus is King obviously doesn't come naturally in this world. If it did, everyone would be doing it, and this series would be unnecessary.

"REPENTANCE & TRANSFORMATION" is all about the "How." In the course of everyday life, how can we actually live the kind of life envisioned throughout the New Testament? How can we be "about the King's business"? How can we abide in Jesus Christ? And perhaps most importantly, how can we become the kind of people for whom such a life would be natural?

Repentance
Let's begin our pursuit of the "How" by looking to the beginning of Jesus' ministry in the gospel of Mark:

> The time is fulfilled, and the kingdom of God is at hand; repent and believe in the gospel.
> – Jesus (Mark 1:15)

There's a common misconception that the gospel is something like this: "Be sorry for the bad stuff you've done and accept Jesus' forgiveness and you can go to heaven when you die." Obviously, this is a different "gospel" than what Jesus announced. In this alternative, repentance has been replaced with remorse and God's kingdom replaced with forgiveness and heaven. But to understand the "How" of new life in

Jesus Christ, we must begin with a better understanding of repentance. Here are two primary aspects of repentance that are formative for this study:

1. **Rethinking** – A new way of thinking & perceiving based on what has taken place: the nearness of God's kingdom in and through Jesus Christ. A new worldview.
2. **Responding** – A new way of living because of the circumstances in which you now find yourself – Jesus has become King, and the full manifestation of his kingdom is on the way.

Here's how we might paraphrase Mark 1:15 to better understand repentance in the context of Jesus' gospel:

> "God's plan is getting back on track. I'm becoming King. So you're going to have to RETHINK everything and learn to live differently in RESPONSE to the circumstances in which you now find yourself."

Transformation

In Romans 12, we find the same exhortation from Paul: rethink & respond. Except now, the mind and body are called into action in the context of worship and transformation:

> I appeal to you, brothers, by the mercies of God, to present your bodies as a living sacrifice, holy and acceptable to God, which is your spiritual worship. Do not be conformed to this world, but be transformed by the renewal of your mind, that by testing you may discern what is the will of God, what is good and acceptable and perfect.
> – Paul (Romans 12:1-2)

Rethinking & responding...this is how new life in Jesus begins. This is also how it continues. Christian faith isn't about a religious experience.

It's about awakening to a truer reality. When this happens, things need to change.

As God's people, we are not to be conformed to the way the world thinks and lives. We need transformation. We need renewal in our thinking, perception, and understanding. We need renewal in our daily habits and rhythms of life. This is the ongoing renewal – body & mind together – that Paul recognizes as genuine, spiritual worship.

Rethinking & responding constitute the "How" of living well when Jesus is King. These two elements make up the two-fold approach for each book in the LWWJK series. While they are examined separately below, there is actually a great deal of overlap. The renewal of our minds is necessarily intertwined with learning to offer our bodies – our daily habits and rhythms – to God in worship.

Rethinking
Each week, there is a brief reading with corresponding reflection and engagement questions. The goal is to renew our thinking and sharpen our perception of reality as it unfolds and emerges through the biblical narrative. This progressive renewal of our thinking and imagination fuels our weekly discussions of God's ongoing work in and around us. This weekly rhythm is one way in which we're learning to participate in God's work in and around us.

Responding
Many Christians focus almost entirely on the mental aspects of their faith. Yet Jesus' example with the first disciples is completely holistic. **Before they had any idea of what they had gotten themselves into, the disciples began learning Jesus' habits & rhythms of living.** In fact, they set themselves apart as disciples not by their knowledge, but by their willingness to actually put one foot in front of the other, day after day, to follow Jesus. Along the way, they watched and learned how Jesus directed his physical body in an act of unceasing worship:
- They watched Jesus fast.
- They watched Jesus pray.
- They witnessed Jesus' intimate knowledge of the scriptures.
- They watched Jesus practice silence and solitude unto the Father.
- They celebrated with Jesus.

Reimagining Discipleship

- They served others together.

The first disciples learned to invest their time and energy – through their physical bodies – in the spiritual disciplines/practices modeled by Jesus. They learned to offer their bodies – their daily habits & rhythms – to God in worship. They learned to live differently in response to the circumstances in which they found themselves.

In LWWJK, we will gradually learn to do the same. As we invest ourselves each week in the renewal of our minds, we will also invest some of our limited time and energy into discipleship – embracing Jesus' faith practices as our own and adapting them for our lives here and now.

Through this two-fold approach – rethinking & responding – we'll embrace Jesus' call to repentance and God's chosen method for our ongoing transformation. We'll create space to cooperate with God's ongoing work in and around us. We'll become a new kind of people for whom bearing fruit and going about the King's business is quite natural.

REIMAGINING DISCIPLESHIP: EXPECTATIONS & COMMITMENT

Expectations

Each book has goals & purpose. Each comes with its own expectations & commitments. Here's what you can expect in REDISCOVERING DISCIPLESHIP:

- You'll develop a clearer understanding of the Bible as God's unfolding story and see how Jesus, the Church, and the gospel emerge from within it. This clarity should catalyze an ongoing renewal of your mind. You should begin to see your own life differently as a person living WITHIN God's story.

- You'll gain practical experience with some of the life-shaping habits and rhythms that Jesus modeled and taught to his first disciples. These practices will create space in your life for God to continue his work in you. In short, expect legitimate change. Expect to be transformed.

- Through a clearer understanding of the Bible and the experience you'll gain in the process of discipleship, you'll be equipped and empowered to continue growing as a disciple long after this study ends (if you so choose), and you'll grow significantly in your capacity and confidence to disciple others.

As you read over these expectations, consider briefly what they would be worth to you. What price would you be willing to pay for this to happen in your life? What would you give up for this kind of experience? How much time would you be willing to invest?

There's certainly nothing beyond your grasp about the next 16 weeks together. But it will take some time and effort each day. It will mean letting go of some old ways of thinking and perceiving life in order to submit yourself into something much bigger. It will mean learning to live a life worthy of eternity! Sure – it will cost a little time and energy. Things may change. But the reward is FAR greater than the cost!

Commitment

The intent over the next 4 months is to reorient lives as apprentices of Jesus Christ in order to become the kind of people who are naturally and increasingly "about the King's business." As you consider undertaking this transformational journey, here's the commitment we're making with one another:

- To grow in our faith in Jesus Christ and our confidence in the Bible as God's Word to us.

- To reorient our lives around 16 weekly gatherings. This includes some time 3 different days in advance of each meeting to read the material (2-4 pages), contemplate 1-2 discussion questions, and write out our answers to enrich our discussions once we're gathered together.

- To reorient our daily lives around various practices (habits and rhythms) that the first disciples learned as they were literally learning to follow Jesus in the days of the New Testament.

- To mutually submit ourselves to Jesus Christ and his ongoing work both in and around us.

When you've considered what lies ahead and you're ready to commit yourself, please sign below along with at least two others who will partner with you and share in the upcoming journey.

In anticipation of God's good work that lies ahead, I am committing myself to each of the elements described above.

Participant: _____

And we commit ourselves to encourage, facilitate, and cooperate with God's ongoing work in our brother/sister:

Partner: _____

Partner: _____

Part 1:

What's the Story?

Reimagining Discipleship

INTRODUCTION

Imagine yourself sitting with a good friend at your favorite restaurant. As you're thoroughly enjoying yourselves around your favorite meals, suddenly a man stands up and runs across the room as fast as he can before lowering his shoulder into a total stranger and blasting him to the ground. Shortly thereafter, the police arrive to escort the monstrous villain off to jail for an impending court date.

Now imagine yourself with that same friend enjoying overpriced nachos and a hotdog at a football game. Suddenly, a man takes off at full speed running across the field before lowering his shoulder into a total stranger and blasting him to the ground. The stadium erupts in praise as thousands of adoring fans scream the name of their armored hero.

The difference in our response to the same behavior? Context.

Perhaps you're thinking... "Context, huh? What does context have to do with faith? Jesus? the Bible?"

Everything.

Whether we realize it or not, we're all living our lives based on how we have learned to perceive our context. We make decisions, spend money, develop relationships, and go to work based on our best perception of the story we're each a part of. We determine our values. We establish priorities. We set goals. We work hard to see our story play out to a desired end.

The question we need to ask ourselves at the outset of our journey together – **how well are we discerning the story in which we're taking part?**

For the record, good intentions have nothing to do with it. For example, if we're on a trip to California and start driving east, our good intentions to get to the Pacific Ocean won't help us actually get there. The same is true for life as a whole. Regardless of our good intentions, misperceiving our context can lead us farther and farther from our intended destination.

Over the next four weeks, we're taking a good, hard look at our context. We're stepping back for a broad look at the biblical narrative. We're working to bring our lives into focus relative to God's story as it unfolds throughout the Bible. We want greater clarity and awareness of who we are, where we are, and the story in which we find ourselves.

As a people wanting to live well before God, we begin our journey together by answering this critical question:

"What's the story?"

Reimagining Discipleship

WEEK 1 - PARAMETERS

- Remembering (what God has done).
- Anticipating (what God has yet to do).
- Participating (in his ongoing work in and around us).

"PARAMETERS"

First things first. The Bible is a story. It's not an instruction manual or rule book. It is a narrative with a beginning, a middle, and an ending. It has a problem, a climax, and a resolution. It follows a plot from beginning to end. To be sure, the Bible contains bountiful wisdom on how to live well as people within the story – but that wisdom falls within the confines, the context, of the story itself.

The Bible is the epic to end all epics. It spans from Creation (Genesis 1-2) to New Creation (Revelation 21-22). There are villains and cowards and heroes. There is ruin and redemption. Betrayal and forgiveness. Confusion and clarity. Death and resurrection.

In "What's the Story?", we're going to bring the biblical narrative into much clearer focus. The ebbs and flows of the story will begin to make more sense and have more meaning. The Bible will become easier to understand and remember. Reading it will become increasingly fun and enjoyable and life-giving.

Be encouraged – we have quite the journey ahead of us! We're going to have a great time together! By the grace of God, none of us will ever be the same, and these next four months will be a time worth remembering and celebrating together forever.

Creation. So back to the story... The Bible begins with the creation of everything we know. The universe comes into being at God's direction, by God's power, and according to God's creative intentions. This is the beginning of the story.

New Creation. After many twists & turns and seemingly irrecoverable disaster, the narrative drives ahead to its culmination in the renewal of all creation. In the end, God's creative intentions are not thwarted by sin or death or evil. This story is not one of second-bests or partial defeats. Everything will be renewed and reunited. In other words, God wins. Entirely. Completely. Thoroughly.

Parameters. Creation and the New Creation are the parameters of our story. There's a common Christian sentiment that says, "This world is not my home." But actually, it is! Creation is where God created us to be, and it's where we'll be in the end. For the time being, it is in desperate need of renewal and restoration, but creation has always been God's plan for us.

Being clear about these parameters is the first step in getting our story straight. It's the first step in rightly discerning our context. And it's an important step toward understanding the significance of our lives here & now. Knowing where our story began and where it's heading is the beginning of living well when Jesus is King.

Creation and New Creation define our context. They define the story in which we find ourselves.

THE story.

The ETERNAL story.

GOD's story.

OUR story.

Our lives unfold everyday between Creation & New Creation. Here & now – with every decision, every action, every word, every relationship, every priority – we're taking our places, determining our roles, and defining ourselves for eternity.

Reimagining Discipleship

Day #1: What other "stories" influence the lives of those around you? (What are people living for? What are their hopes and dreams? Who are they hoping to become? How do they perceive the significance of their lives?)

_____

_____

_____

_____

How might the reality of God's story cause people to rethink their hopes and dreams? Their own significance? Their purpose?

_____

_____

_____

_____

Day #2: How is God working in your life lately? How might this reshape your role within God's story?

_____

_____

_____

_____

Day #3: How might you begin to adjust your priorities, relationships, finances, and time management based on the realization that you're already taking your place in God's story based on the life you're living?

_____

_____

_____

_____

_____

DAILY PRACTICES: JESUS' WAY OF LIVING

Over the course of our journey together, we want to submit ourselves to some of the same habits and rhythms that Jesus' first disciples would have learned from him as they literally followed him around Israel about 2,000 years ago. This week, we'll begin one set of practices that will continue for the duration of REIMAGINING DISCIPLESHIP.

Remember that these practices are NOT meritorious efforts. We're NOT trying to earn anything from God. They are ways in which we are creating space for God to speak to us and to work in us, and for us to recognize and participate in God's work in those around us. Each practice is drawn from the example of Jesus and his first disciples. They are means by which we'll present our bodies (not just our thoughts and affections) to God in worship.

Practice #1: "Reorienting" (Bible Reading)

Description: 4 days each week, read 5 chapters from the Old Testament and 5 chapters from the New Testament proceeding from start to finish in each – about 40 chapters total each week. (See "OT Readings" in the Appendix. This modified reading schedule allows for us to finish the biblical narrative within our allotted time together.)

Goal/Purpose: Paul said in Romans 12:2 that we're transformed by the renewal of our minds. Immersing ourselves in the biblical narrative will do just that. As we read, we're leveraging our time and energy in an act of worship & trusting God to accomplish a renewal of our imaginations and worldview. Scripture is a primary way in which God speaks to us. So embracing the discipline of bible reading is simply a means of submitting ourselves to a way God has already chosen to work within us.

Practice #2: "Pages" (Prayer)

Description: 3 days each week, make a one page (minimum) prayer entry into a dedicated notebook.

Goal/Purpose: Hand-writing our prayers to God will promote our transformation in several ways. First, it forces us to slow down, be still, and learn how to be with God without the numbing distractions of FB, smart-phones, technology, TV, etc. Second, hand-writing prayers teaches us to vulnerably, coherently, and intentionally give ourselves to God – our concerns, our joys, our hopes, our fears - everything.

Reimagining Discipleship

CONNECT
Over the coming week, how can we support, encourage, celebrate and pray for each other?

_____

_____

_____

_____

_____

_____

CLOSING PRAYER
Remembering.
Anticipating.
Participating.

PARAMETERS: Notes & Reflections

_____

_____

_____

_____

_____

_____

_____

_____

_____

_____

_____

_____

_____

WEEK 2 - FLOW

OPENING PRAYER: Remembering. Anticipating. Participating.

FOLLOW-UP

How did the first week of reading and prayer practices go?

_____

_____

_____

What challenges did you face? What successes can we celebrate?

_____

_____

_____

How did you recognize God speaking/working in and around you this past week as a result of your practices?

_____

_____

_____

Were you able to reimagine/reconsider any circumstances or decisions this past week because of an increased awareness of your life's broader context between Creation (Genesis 1-2) & New Creation (Revelation 21-22)? Please explain.

_____

_____

_____

"FLOW"

God's story is our story. It's our true context. It began long before us. Its culmination has yet to unfold. As people living between Genesis 1-2 and Revelation 21-22, we're taking our places within God's story. Through the lives we're now living, we're defining ourselves before God for all eternity.

But as a people intending to live well within God's story, we need to know more about our context than just its beginning and ending. So this week, we turn our attention to the flow of God's story. To do so, let's imagine flipping through our bibles from Genesis 1 to Revelation 22. Here's a summary of the story that emerges:

> A. Creation
> > B. Israel
> > > C. Jesus Christ
> > B'. Church
> A'. New Creation

Reflexive & Progressive

This overview introduces us to two aspects of the flow of the biblical narrative. First, God's story is reflexive. The first half of the story is mirrored by the second. New Creation is an echo and culmination of Creation. The Church echoes and culminates God's purposes in and through Israel. And everything hinges on Jesus.

The reflexive aspect of God's story has to do with its REDEMPTIVE nature. Following the beauty and wonder of Creation, there's a disastrous mess: rebellion, tragedy, death, evil. But amidst the chaos and destruction, the story presses ahead. A mission gets underway. A divine mission. A redemptive mission. God's purposes are not abandoned. They will be restored.

Naturally, the story reaches its apex in Jesus Christ - THE REDEEMER. But Jesus wasn't trying to recreate Genesis 1-2. God's plan was moving forward. And this brings us to the second aspect of the flow – God's story is progressive. It's going somewhere. It's pressing ahead. In Jesus, the downward spiral ended. Death was defeated. Renewal began in Jesus' resurrection, and its fullness is now anticipated by the rest of creation. (This is the story Paul is telling in Romans 8 and 1 Corinthians 15.)

In other words, through the life, death, and resurrection of Jesus Christ, God's redemptive story is now progressing toward its culmination in the New Creation.

Scope and Trajectory
Now let's rearrange our summary and draw out two more aspects of the flow of God's story: scope & trajectory.

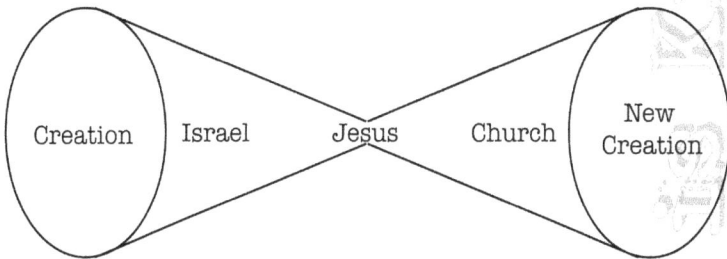

Creation. Our story begins with a boundless scope. It encompasses all of creation. All humanity is created and called according to God's purposes. Creation is designed to roll forward in eternal rhythms free from decay and death.

In the fall, the eternal rhythms of Creation were interrupted and cut short by death. The wholeness of Creation was severed, and a veil came to exist between the heavenly and earthly realms. Humanity forfeited its God-given identity and purpose in favor of selfishness & rebellion. The trajectory of God's story became defined by rebellion, destruction, and ruin.

Israel. After the fall, the redemptive mission of God quickly got underway with the calling of Abraham (Genesis 12). With Abraham's calling, the scope of God's story narrowed to the land, the people, and the history of Abraham's descendants – Israel.

Unfortunately, instead of living into God's redemptive purposes, the nation of Israel fell to the same fate as humanity in Creation – rebellion and selfishness. The narrowing, downward spiral of failure, destruction, and ruin continued.

Jesus Christ. Finally, the story collapsed from all of Creation onto one life, one moment, one place. The power of sin, evil, and destruction culminated at the cross when Jesus was crucified. Perfect love and goodness was taken to the grave. The trajectory of rebellion and evil ran its course.

But just as all seemed to be lost, the unthinkable happened! The story turned. The Jesus was resurrected! New Creation dawned!

And now, from one man, an empty grave, and the first breath of resurrection life, God's story is exploding back out toward the renewal of all things.

Church. This expanding scope and redemptive trajectory now define God's story and contextualize God's people living between Jesus and the New Creation. While much of humanity continues to live in opposition to God's purposes, the Church is taking its place as followers of Jesus Christ here & now: announcing the good news that God's story is back on track through Jesus Christ and living beyond ourselves as cooperative participants in God's ongoing redemptive mission.

New Creation. Ultimately, all creation will be renewed under the reign of Jesus Christ and his people. Through God's righteous judgment, all people will assume their rightful places before Jesus & within God's kingdom. Jesus' victory over death & destruction will be shared by all his people as they step fully into eternal life in the New Creation.

RETHINKING & RESPONDING

Day #1: In your own words, describe the flow of God's story.

_____

_____

_____

_____

What about the flow of God's story constitutes "good news"?

_____

_____

_____

_____

Day #2: What aspects of your life could be better aligned with the redemptive flow of God's story (living beyond yourself in anticipation of complete renewal & restoration)? What might that look like?

_____

_____

_____

_____

Day #3: What steps could you take to increasingly live beyond yourself for the sake of others in your relationships, time management, and finances?

_____

_____

_____

_____

_____

Reimagining Discipleship

Last week, we adapted two disciplines into our daily, 21st century lives that were evident in the lives of Jesus and his earliest disciples. This is one way of offering our bodies to God in worship (Romans 12:1) & submitting ourselves into the process of discipleship unto Jesus Christ.

As we noted last week, these practices are NOT meritorious efforts before God. They are ways in which we are creating space for God to speak to us and to work in us, and for us to recognize and participate in the good work God is doing in those around us.

This week (and for the duration of our journey through REIMAGINING DISCIPLESHIP), we'll continue:

Practice #1: "Reorienting" (Bible Reading)
Practice #2: "Pages" (Prayer)

We're also adding a practice that is perhaps most often recounted in the life of Jesus:

Practice #3: "Present to God" (Silence & Solitude)
There are numerous times in the gospels that Jesus stepped away from ministry and the company of others to set himself apart unto God. He disappeared into the night. He journeyed to lonely mountainsides. He escaped noise and commotion in favor of silence and solitude with the Father.

On the contrary, many people today are addicted to distraction. We maintain constant media exposure (TV, radio, internet). We lack focus. We dread stillness. We can hardly endure more than a few consecutive moments of quiet. We have forgotten how to be fully present...to anyone. For you and me, this is about to change! As Jesus' followers today, we're going to begin adapting and embracing Jesus' life-shaping habits of silence & solitude that we might become increasingly present to God.

Description: Every day, set aside 20 minutes to be in silence & solitude in order to practice being fully present to God. This may be extremely difficult at first. Your thoughts may race and wander. You may squirm and suffer...but press on! This is an act of worship. God will begin working and speaking. You're embracing a course of transformation. Be encouraged and press on!

Goal: To become the kind of person who is naturally, increasingly, and directly present to God. To become free from the need for numbness & distraction – whether through smart phones and media or even through dynamic preaching and soul-warming worship music.

CONNECT
Over the coming week, how can we support, encourage, celebrate, and pray for each other?

_____

_____

_____

_____

_____

_____

CLOSING PRAYER
Remembering.
Anticipating.
Participating.

FLOW: Notes & Reflections

_____

_____

_____

_____

_____

_____

_____

Reimagining Discipleship

WEEK #3 - PERSPECTIVE

OPENING PRAYER: Remembering. Anticipating. Participating.

FOLLOW-UP

How did the daily practices go this week?

_____

_____

Have these practices helped you discern God speaking to you or recognize his work in someone around you? How?

_____

_____

_____

In what person near you do you think God may be working?

_____

How could you cooperate with what God is doing?

_____

_____

_____

Think back over your week. Did anything take place that you need to reimagine in light of your place within God's story? How does that circumstance take on a new light within God's story?

_____

_____

_____

_____

_____

"EMPHASES"

As we embark on our third week together, hopefully God's story is beginning to stick in the back of our minds – reshaping our perspectives and refocusing our worldview. Hopefully we're beginning to reimagine ourselves within God's story. And hopefully, by the grace of God, we're beginning to learn to align our time, our relationships, our finances, and our pursuits with the trajectory of God's story.

Last week, we looked at the flow of God's story. What becomes quickly apparent is that the whole story hinges on Jesus. In and through Jesus, the trajectory and flow turned from spiraling disaster to epic redemption and renewal.

Despite the magnitude of God's story, it's not always easy to maintain perspective in the course of everyday life. Sometimes it gets lost in the face of life's circumstances. Other times, we get so focused on particular points of emphasis within God's story that we "lose the forest for the trees."

This week, we're going to consider two such points of emphasis with the intention of submitting them back into the context of the broader biblical narrative. Before we do, let's review the story with an eye toward Jesus' perspective within the biblical narrative.

When Jesus stepped into God's story, here's how he announced that which was taking place:

> **"The kingdom of God is now within reach –
> God's reign is unfolding. You're going to
> have to rethink...everything...and respond
> accordingly in the way that you're living."
> (Mark 1:15 paraphrase)**

The meaning of Jesus' announcement is easily lost apart from an awareness of the broader story in which the announcement came. This wasn't a religious declaration. It wasn't just for Israel. And it wasn't just about something taking place off in the heavens. Jesus was announcing the restoration of God's reign over creation. Everything was changing. Forever.

Jesus stood as the apex between Creation and the New Creation. He looked back at a time when all things existed in unity and wholeness according to God's plan. Despite the stranglehold of chaos and rebellion, he didn't turn away from creation. The Redeemer came. Everything changed.

Through the life, death, and resurrection of Jesus Christ, God's story turned from ruin to restoration. Although his victory has yet to be fully implemented, the rebellion has been crushed. Sin, corruption, and death are defeated and no longer have dominion over Creation. God's reign over creation has been re-established in and through Jesus Christ. This is some great news!

This is God's story. But like any story, if we focus too much on particular details, we lose perspective. When that happens, the true significance of the details themselves often gets lost. It's then that they can take on a life of their own within the smaller stories of various religious and social contexts.

Let's consider two common emphases in God's story. They are worth noting both because of their prevalence and because of their tendency to shape people's worldviews apart from the fuller context of God's story.

#1 – Human/Earthly Emphasis. Many Christians focus on the human aspects of God's story. They rightly discern humanity's important role in creation. They emphasize Jesus' incarnation (humanity), his moral/ethical teachings, and his example of love and compassion. Their faith often manifests itself in good works – caring for the poor, feeding the hungry, and the promotion of general human welfare.

But this focus needs to be kept in perspective. When it's lost, the human/earthly details take on a life of their own. Compared to Jesus' gospel announcement in Mark 1:15, the story has changed: The promise of universal human welfare subtly replaces God's reign as the focus and hope of the good news. The kingdom of God is reduced to human accomplishment. And repentance becomes a matter of embracing the correct political & social agendas rather than living in submission and obedience to a coming king.

Obviously, this human/earthly emphasis can become too narrow. It must always be interpreted within the context of God's story where redemption goes far beyond human vision & attainment:

- All of creation – the heavens and the earth together – will one day be reunited & whole according to God's original intentions. Death & sickness will not just be scientifically resisted. They will be defeated.
- Most importantly, Jesus is not just a model citizen of the coming kingdom. He is the King.
- Ultimately, humanity will transition into the kingdom based on our relationship to the King – as faithful servants or as rebellious opponents.

#2 – Spiritual/Heavenly Emphasis. For many other Christians, the emphasis is very heavenly. The focus is on Jesus' divinity. These Christians are keenly aware that the world is not as it should be. Their hope lies in heaven. Their faith manifests itself in the desire for people to go to heaven through the forgiveness of sin provided by Jesus on the cross.

This emphasis also needs to be kept in perspective. Otherwise, the story once again changes: Forgiveness and heaven, rather than God's reign, become the hope of the good news. The kingdom of God is restricted to a heavenly/spiritual paradise. And repentance becomes a matter of attaining forgiveness rather than living in submission and obedience to a coming king.

A heavenly focus can easily become too narrow. God's story is much bigger:

- Being dead in heaven isn't the end of our story. All of creation will be renewed – the heavens and the earth together. Decay and death will not prevail.
- Jesus is not just a gate keeper through whom we acquire passage into heaven. He is the King of all Creation.
- Finally, God's kingdom will not be populated with those who successfully acquired forgiveness, but by faithful, repentant servants who embraced the authority of the King and lived in submission and obedience for the time they were given (Luke 19).

Maintaining Perspective

It is worth noting that anytime there is too narrow a focus on particular details of God's story, the meaning of Jesus' gospel is compromised. **And when we lose perspective, Jesus always becomes something less than the reigning King before whom we're living each and every day with eternal implications.**

As Jesus' followers today, we need our hearts and imaginations to be captured by the whole story. We need to see things the way Jesus did. We need to maintain perspective:

- JESUS IS THE KING (Luke 19).

- The heavenly and earthly realms of creation will someday be fully reunited. God and his people will dwell together and reign over the New Creation (Revelation 21-22).

- Jesus' immortality – his resurrection life – has already dawned and will someday be shared with all of his people (1 Corinthians 15).

- As Jesus' followers, we are to live repentantly – rethinking old perspectives & priorities while living in anticipation of our King's return.

A kingdom has been inaugurated. It's within reach. It's time to rethink some things. It's time to live in response. Because this is our story. Because we're already living out our lives **when Jesus is King**.

RETHINKING & RESPONDING

Day #1: What details of God's story do the people in your life tend to emphasize?

_____

_____

Describe how these details fit into God's larger story.

_____

_____

_____

_____

Day #2: Describe the implications of Jesus being the King for our lives here & now. How is this different than if Jesus were only a "model citizen" or a "gate keeper"?

_____

_____

_____

_____

_____

Day #3: Are there areas in your life in which you struggle to maintain perspective? What steps could you take to cooperate with God and grow in these areas?

_____

_____

_____

_____

_____

_____

Reimagining Discipleship

So far, we've adapted three disciplines evident in the life of Jesus and have incorporated them into our daily routines as his disciples here & now.

These practices are ways in which we create space for God to speak to us & work in us and for us to learn to recognize and participate in the good work God is doing in those around us.

Obviously, God CAN work in us however he wants. But these practices are ways that God has CHOSEN to work in & through us. These are practices that the earliest disciples would naturally have learned as they followed Jesus and learned his habits and rhythms of life and ministry.

This week, we'll continue:
Practice #1: "Reorienting" (Bible Reading)
Practice #2: "Pages" (Prayer)
Practice #3: "Present to God" (Silence & Solitude)

And we're adding one of our final two recurring practices:

Practice #4: "Present to Others" (Media/Technology Abstention)
Description: Limit your use of media & technology in order to be fully present to those around you. Talk with your group about the best application of this practice for your own circumstances. Meal times could be a great place to start. Or while enjoying a nice cup of coffee. Or perhaps during bed-time. Turn off the TV and the smart phones. Learn to be free from social media updates. Don't be halfway checked out from those around you. Be present. Learn to be together.
Goal: To be fully present to those around us. Ultimately, we're not going to be very good at loving others when we're habitually distracted and numb toward those around us. Jesus stepped out of heaven in order to be fully present to us. As his disciples, the least we can do is turn off our stuff to do the same.

CONNECT
Over the coming week, how can we support, encourage, celebrate, and pray for each other?

_____

_____

_____

_____

_____

_____

CLOSING PRAYER
Remembering.
Anticipating.
Participating.

PERSPECTIVE: Notes & Reflections

_____

_____

_____

_____

_____

_____

_____

_____

_____

_____

_____

_____

_____

_____

WEEK 4 - INEVITABILITY

Remembering. Anticipating. Participating.

FOLLOW-UP
How has God been speaking/working in and around you this past week?

_____

_____

_____

How did last week's practices go?

_____

_____

_____

What challenges did you face? What successes can we celebrate?

_____

_____

_____

Are you getting more comfortable being present to God and others (and free from the need for distractions)?

_____

_____

_____

What has it been like to be still and fully present to God and others?

_____

_____

_____

"INEVITABILITY"

Over the past three weeks, we've taken a very broad look at God's story. At Jesus' story. At the human story. At our story.

This week, we want to look at two parables in which Jesus conveyed his perspective from WITHIN the story to his followers. In each parable, Jesus was helping his followers understand how people inevitably take their places within God's story. He was also conveying something of God's expectations for his people.

These particular parables were chosen as representative samples of Jesus' teaching because they frame his earthly ministry. Mark 4 is Jesus' first parable and Luke 19 among his last. While they're certainly unique from one another, it is easy to see that they also hold much in common – much that we should take to heart.

Mark 4:1-20. (Read it.) Some things should get our attention right from the start. First, this is Jesus' inaugural teaching in Mark. And when the Son of God comes to earth and decides to start teaching, we better listen up! Second, Jesus indicates that this parable is the "secret of the kingdom of God" (4:11). Again – probably worth paying attention here. Finally, in case there's anyone not yet clued in, Jesus continues, "Do you not understand this parable? How then will you understand all the parables?" (4:13).

Ok, Lord. We're listening...

Parables were not intended to serve as systematic theologies. They don't speak to any and every circumstance. But they drive home specific points very, VERY powerfully. Here's how Jesus began his teaching ministry in Mark 4:

- There are many reasons that seeds don't bear fruit. Most of them occur naturally in the course of "normal" life.

- From God's perspective, there are really only two kinds of seeds – those that bear fruit and those that do not. And most do not.

- It's the fruit bearing (or lack thereof) that truly defines us. Not hearing God's word. Not good intentions. Not affection or sentimentality. Only fruit.

This is the teaching with which Jesus saw fit to inaugurate his ministry. And it appears from the other gospels (Matthew 13 & Luke 8) that Jesus told this same parable repeatedly. As he went around proclaiming and manifesting the good news of God's kingdom, Jesus clearly wanted people to understand that they were already defining themselves before God based on the fruit they were (or weren't) producing.

Luke 19:11-27. (Read it.) In this parable, Jesus still hasn't gotten past the whole "kingdom" thing. He started there, and he stuck with it to the end.

Once again, the context of the passage is worth noting: Jesus and the disciples are heading to Jerusalem, and the disciples mistakenly assume that the kingdom is to appear immediately. Jesus tells the parable to warn them of the impending delay in his return and more importantly that they would define themselves in his eternal kingdom by the lives they lived as they awaited his return.

Then & now, there are 3 stereotypical responses to Jesus' claim of Lordship over our lives:
- Outright opposition and defiance.
- Cautious, subtle denial.
- Whole-hearted embrace and obedient service.

Then & now, here's the point...
Our place in Jesus' eternal kingdom is determined by our response to him – how we go about our business day by day. And our response is inevitable. The people in the parable didn't have a choice as to whether or not they would be included in the story. Their circumstances were thrust upon them. Their only decision was HOW they would respond. The same is true for us today.

There's a common sentiment in the world today...
People want nothing to do with Jesus.
But according to Jesus, that's not an option.
Like it or not, everyone has a place in God's story.

A Word of Caution...
Many people in this world oppose the notion that Jesus would reign over them. This opposition is innate to American culture. Our country is founded on individual rights, independence, and democracy. If left unchallenged, these cultural values can shape even American "Christians" to resist the idea that Jesus reigns over them. While such people may be great fans of Jesus, they have no intention of Jesus reigning over their relationships, time, money, and priorities.

Many others aren't so sure about things. They express a much more subtle denial of Jesus' lordship. This group will undoubtedly be somewhat religious. They are, after all, playing it safe. If & when they do encounter Jesus, they don't want to be exposed as enemies of his kingdom. But their lives aren't shaped by a strong sense of anticipation, and they certainly don't want to give up their time, money, and personal interests – while potentially inviting the scorn and animosity of regular "citizens" – by identifying too closely with Jesus and dedicating their lives to serving his purposes.

Finally, there are faithful servants who live in confident anticipation of the king's return. He shapes their identity, and they willingly put their lives on the line in service of his kingdom even while its full manifestation is yet to be seen.

This is how Jesus saw things. This is how he wanted us to see things, too. This is the true human context. Like it or not, we're all a part of this story. Inclusion is inevitable. The only real question: Who will we be? How will we emerge within God's story?

And Jesus was clear: we're already deciding. With every relationship. With our time and our money. We're revealing our allegiance to the King and taking our places in his eternal kingdom.

Reimagining Discipleship

RETHINKING & RESPONDING

Day #1: Looking back at Mark 4, where/how is the "fruit" of your life most likely to be interrupted?

_____

_____

What areas of your life are the most difficult to submit to the Lordship of Jesus Christ? Why?

_____

_____

_____

Day #2: Think back over the various ways God has worked in your life and the seeds that he has planted over the years. Now imagine all of those seeds suddenly breaking through and bearing fruit. Describe how your life would be changing and what it would be like:

_____

_____

_____

_____

_____

_____

Day #3: Look at your notes from yesterday. What's holding you back from this kind of life? Is the reward worth the cost?

_____

_____

What opportunities are around you right now to participate in "the King's business"?

_____

_____

_____

DAILY PRACTICES: JESUS' WAY OF LIVING

Over the past several weeks, we've been increasingly and intentionally leveraging our time and energy to cooperate with God's ongoing work in and around us. We've been embracing the habits and rhythms of discipleship.

Hopefully by now, we're each noticing a subtle transformation underway. Practices that once required great focus and effort have begun to feel natural and life-giving. Whereas practicing our faith was once out of the ordinary, perhaps it is now coming to define us.

If so, this is a transformation worth celebrating! You've begun learning a new way of life. You've started down a path that has no limit. God's work in and around you will continue to deepen and progress to the degree you're willing to follow. Praise God! Keep up the good work.

This week, let's continue building on what we've begun:
Practice #1: "Reorienting" (Bible Reading)
Practice #2: "Pages" (Prayer)
Practice #3: "Present to God" (Silence & Solitude)
Practice #4: "Present to Others" (Media/tech. Abstention)

And now let's add our final recurring practice for REIMAGINING DISCIPLESHIP:

Practice #5: "Re-Sourcing" (24/36hr. Fasting)
Description: Fasting is an age-old practice for Christians. Jesus talked about it and practiced it. Fasting is simply abstaining from food for a given period of time. Oftentimes, Christians will go on extended fasts for particular reasons. In the present case, we're practicing weekly fasting in the interest of general transformation and life-shaping. For the duration of this study, we'll each pick a day of the week and engage in either a 24 or 36 hour fast. (Obviously, 24 = dinner to dinner while 36 = dinner to breakfast 36 hours later.)(In rare cases, it may be necessary to modify this practice for medical reasons. Please do so as needed.)
Goal: We're primarily learning to embrace God as our source. Additionally, fasting increases our capacity to deny even our most basic desires and impulses in order to submit them to God.

Reimagining Discipleship

<u>CONNECT</u>
Over the coming week, how can we support, encourage, celebrate and pray for each other?

_____

_____

_____

_____

_____

_____

<u>CLOSING PRAYER</u>
Remembering.
Anticipating.
Participating.

<u>PERSPECTIVE</u>: Notes & Reflections

_____

_____

_____

_____

_____

_____

_____

_____

_____

_____

_____

_____

_____

_____

Part 2:

Who is Jesus?

Reimagining Discipleship

We began our journey together with an important question: "What's the Story?" In response, we invested 4 weeks examining the biblical narrative as it plays out from Creation to New Creation. During that time, we grew much more aware of God's story as OUR story: We are a people within the narrative looking back on Jesus' resurrection and ahead to the New Creation.

At this point, some things should be quite clear. First, the story in which we're taking part is FAR bigger than us. This is important to keep in mind as we're about the business of our daily lives – hectic schedules, jobs, bills, grocery shopping, family activities, marriage, and parenting. When life grinds us down and obscures our perspective, the Bible reminds us that we're part of something that is anything but mundane or ordinary.

Second, the lives we're living matter. Profoundly. God created us in his own image and to share in his purposes. He invites us here & now to take part in his ongoing redemptive mission. As followers of Jesus, we're learning to go about the business of God's kingdom and live in anticipation of the day when Jesus' redemptive victory will overtake all of creation.

Finally, God's story encompasses ALL people. Inclusion is inevitable: as defiant rebels, as reluctant servants waiting to see if Jesus is actually going to be King, or as faithful servants being groomed to reign with Jesus in the New Creation. (Now that's a refreshing and jarring thought as I sit here writing on an early Monday morning before heading out into a stressful work week!)

Here's another exciting thought as we transition into Part 2: This isn't just our story. **This is Jesus' story, too.**

Unfortunately, too many people are unaware of the sweeping biblical narrative and therefore fail to recognize much of Jesus' meaning and significance. For many, Jesus just appeared in Bethlehem all those years ago like a bolt of divine lightning. He was a nice guy we should all try to emulate. He was very loving & kind. And then, he died on a cross so that people could hear about him, be forgiven, and go to heaven when they die. But that's about the extent of most people's awareness of the most significant person in history...

Practically speaking, our knowledge of Jesus often doesn't go much beyond that of many other biblical heroes. We know cool stories about what Jesus did and accomplished...and Moses. And Elijah. And David. And Joshua. And Esther. And Paul...

But Jesus certainly wasn't like the other biblical heroes. Moses did AMAZING things. Elijah raised people from the dead and even ascended into heaven. Even so, no one thought that one of these two Old Testament heroes was God. So following his Damascus road experience (recounted in Acts 9), what did Paul recognize was taking place in and around Jesus that led him to such previously blasphemous conclusions: Jesus was God; the Temple system was now obsolete; the Jew/Gentile barrier was gone; it was time to take the gospel beyond the borders of Israel to the whole world. Paul's response begs the questions,

"**Who is Jesus?**"
"**How does he fit into God's story?**"

Four weeks ago, we started our journey with a broad look at God's story. Now, we begin zooming in to see who Jesus is and how he fits within it. Along the way, we'll answer some important questions:

- Why did Jesus need to come as a human?
- Why did Jesus come as an Israelite?
- Why did Paul come to the conclusion that Jesus was God?
- What in the world does "Messiah"/"Christ" mean? And what led people to conclude that was who Jesus was?

On the other side of "Who is Jesus?", we'll emerge with a much more robust understanding of Jesus. We'll emerge with greater appreciation for just how ridiculously amazing he is. And we'll understand how God's whole redemptive plan came together in him.

WEEK 5 - THE SON OF MAN

<u>OPENING PRAYER</u>: (3 volunteers)
Remembering (what God has done).
Anticipating (what God has yet to do).
Participating (in his ongoing work in and around us).

<u>FOLLOW-UP</u>

What are the 3 most significant things you'll take away from Part 1?

1. _____

2. _____

3. _____

After four weeks, what are your reflections on the practices we've been implementing? Have they created space for God's work in you?

_____

_____

_____

_____

After four weeks looking at the biblical narrative, has your perspective on any of your circumstances changed? How?

_____

_____

_____

_____

What opportunities have arisen in the course of your everyday life to be a faithful servant "about the King's business"?

_____

_____

_____

"HUMANITY"

Most Christians know that the incarnation of Jesus is a big deal...for some reason. Most know that he came to show us how to love others. Most know that he came to die for our sins. But our understanding of the significance of Jesus' life and ministry tends to fade out quickly beyond his compassion & crucifixion and our corresponding forgiveness.

If that's all there is to know, we're left with a lot of questions. For example, why did God give us the Old Testament (and most of the New Testament) instead of just a few isolated tales of Jesus' compassion and then his crucifixion? In the gospels, why did Jesus talk about everything in terms of a "kingdom"? And why is the New Testament so focused on resurrection when it was through the crucifixion that our sins were forgiven?

After spending four weeks looking at the broader biblical context of Jesus' life and ministry, it should be clear that he didn't step out of heaven just to get himself crucified so we could all go back to heaven. During his earthly ministry, Jesus proclaimed and manifested good news that went far beyond "Be forgiven. Be good. Be with me when you're dead."

Jesus became human to enter into a story that began long before his incarnation. Much had already transpired. Much needed to be done. Much was in store for humanity and all of creation. So when the time was just right...

the Word became flesh and blood, and moved into the neighborhood. John 1:14 (MSG)

Let's turn once again into God's story - this time in pursuit of a greater, deeper, more profound appreciation and understanding of Jesus: the Son of Man, the Son of David, the Son of God, the Messiah.

The Beginning. Beyond the evolution debate and Sunday school lessons for the kiddos, there is a tendency in church life to move past Genesis 1-2 without much thought. But what if we slowed down and actually paid attention to what was happening in Creation? What was God setting in motion? What were God's original intentions for humanity? And most pointedly:

If Jesus is the REDEEMER, what scenario is he redeeming?

God's Purposes for Humanity. According to Genesis 1-2, God's creative intentions for human life revolved around three intertwined elements:

- THE BLESSING OF GOD. On the heels of their creation, God's first act was to bless humanity (Gen. 1:28). He intended humanity to live as a blessed people before him. This blessing defined God's original context for humanity.
- THE KNOWLEDGE OF GOD. Humanity was also created to live in the knowledge of God. The fullness of this divine intention does not emerge in the creation narrative until near its end. Genesis 3:8-10 reveals that people knew God in a manner hard for us to imagine: Adam and Eve recognized the sound of God walking in the garden with them and (it seems) audibly heard God calling to them. God's intention was never to be separated from his people. His plan was to dwell with humanity amidst a whole creation without the veil that now lies between the heavens and the earth.
- THE REIGN OF GOD. God chose to reign over his creation through his governors – men & women. As his image-bearers, they would reflect his character and beauty throughout Creation as they governed it on his behalf (Genesis 1:26-27). Through this divine-human cooperative effort, all Creation was to continue to grow and develop in a state of God's blessing (Genesis 1:28-30).

The Fall. When humanity rebelled against God's order and purposes for Creation, the fallout was catastrophic. We colluded in the dominion of evil. All creation became subject to the consequences of our selfishness & rebellion. God's blessed creation was marred by the curse of sin and evil. The knowledge of God faded. A veil came to separate the heavenly and earthly realms of creation. And people forgot what it was like to walk with God.

The Son of Man. It was into this dark scene that Jesus came. Into God's story. Into the midst of fallen humanity. Into the midst of a broken Creation. The Redeemer came. The Son of Man moved into the neighborhood.

For God's story to get back on track, humanity needed redemption. We rebelled. We failed. But Jesus didn't. In him, we (humanity) were faithful to God's creative intentions.

As the Son of Man, Jesus stepped into God's story to REPRESENT and REDEEM humanity:

- THE BLESSING OF GOD. Through Jesus' life, death, and resurrection, all Creation has been blessed and presses forward on a trajectory toward complete restoration and renewal.
- THE KNOWLEDGE OF GOD. In Jesus, God was revealed and made known (John 14:9 & Colossians 1:19).
- THE REIGN OF GOD. Jesus submitted himself to the purposes and reign of the Father – and became the King of kings and Lord of lords (Philippians 2:5-11).

Jesus' humanity was not lost on the New Testament authors. They were highly aware of God's story and Jesus' place within it. For example, notice how the following passages renew the human story in and through Jesus:

Temptation (Matthew 4 & Luke 4). The ministry of Jesus is inaugurated in the synoptic gospels (Matthew, Mark and Luke) by Jesus' baptism and subsequent temptation. But unlike Adam and Eve, who succumbed to temptation, Jesus remained faithfully submitted to God. The human story was renewed.

The Garden (John 18-20). Near the end of his gospel, John carefully echoes the Creation narrative just as God's story turned from disaster to the dawning of the New Creation. The ultimate culmination of sin and evil at the cross began as Jesus and his disciples entered THE GARDEN (John 18:1). Then, as the New Creation dawned in Jesus' resurrection, Jesus was mistaken to be the GARDENER (John 20:15). So, John subtly reminds us – Creation fell at the hands of humanity in the garden. And in another garden, it was redeemed.

"like God" (Philippians 2:5-11). Where Adam rebelled and grasped at the possibility to be like God, Jesus faithfully submitted himself and laid down his life.

Adam (Romans 5:12-21; 1 Corinthians 15:21-22). In two of the most direct Jesus/Adam comparisons, Paul explicitly names Jesus as a "new" Adam. Whereas Adam set humanity on a trajectory of sin and death, through Jesus came righteousness, resurrection, and renewal.

Humanity was created with a central role in Creation. After the fall, we needed redeemed if God's story was to get back on track. So the Redeemer came as the Son of Man. As a man, Jesus faithfully represented humanity. Through him, God's people look forward to the fullness of our own redemption when Jesus returns and we take our places under him: sharing God's blessing and likeness everywhere, living in the unabated knowledge of God, and reigning over the New Creation.

RETHINKING & RESPONDING

Day #1: In your own words, recap the significance and purpose of humanity based on the Creation account in Genesis:

_____

_____

_____

_____

_____

Why did Jesus need to come as a human?

_____

_____

_____

_____

Day #2: How do God's intentions and purposes for humanity affect your own self-worth and perception?

_____

_____

_____

_____

_____

Day #3: How might your life change as God's original intentions for you are increasingly redeemed through the ongoing work of Jesus Christ in you?

_____

_____

_____

_____

_____

Reimagining Discipleship

DAILY PRACTICES: JESUS' WAY OF LIVING

Over the course of our journey together, we're submitting ourselves to some of the same habits and rhythms that Jesus' first disciples would have learned as they literally followed Jesus around Israel about 2,000 years ago.

These practices are NOT meritorious efforts before God. They are ways in which we are creating space for God to speak to us and to work in us, and for us to recognize and participate in the good work God is doing in those around us. They are drawn from the example of Jesus and his first disciples. Finally, they are means by which we present our bodies (not just our thoughts and affections) to God in worship.

Here's a review of our recurring practices:

Practice #1: "Reorienting" (Bible Reading)
Practice #2: "Pages" (Prayer)
Practice #3: "Present to God" (Silence & Solitude)
Practice #4: "Present to Others" (Media/tech Abstention)
Practice #5: "Re-Sourcing" (24/36 Fasting)

And finally...
Practice #6: "Psalm 23" (Memorization & Meditation)
For the duration of PART 2: WHO IS JESUS?, we'll be memorizing Psalm 23 and learning to meditate upon it (to hold it in our thoughts) in the course of daily life.

As the passage is committed to memory, we'll practice intentionally recalling its verses in the face of challenging circumstances in order to rethink & respond as a people living under the watchful eye of our good Shepherd.

CONNECT

Over the coming week, how can we support, encourage, celebrate, and pray for each other?

_____

_____

_____

_____

_____

_____

CLOSING PRAYER

Remembering.

Anticipating.

Participating.

HUMANITY: Notes & Reflections

_____

_____

_____

_____

_____

_____

_____

_____

_____

_____

_____

_____

_____

_____

_____

_____

WEEK 6 - THE SON OF DAVID

<u>OPENING PRAYER</u>:
Remembering.
Anticipating.
Participating.

<u>FOLLOW-UP</u>
How is the memorization of Psalm 23 proceeding? (If anyone has it memorized, please recite it for the group. Either this week or in the weeks to come, each person should have the opportunity to recite the passage to the group.)

Have you been able to hold Psalm 23 in your thoughts in order to reconsider any circumstances this week?

_____

_____

_____

How did the rest of your practices go? How have your daily practices created space for God to speak and work in and around you?

_____

_____

_____

Who are 3 people around you in whom you're confident God is at work?

_____

_____

_____

How could you cooperate with what God is doing?

_____

_____

_____

"ISRAEL"

As the story got underway in Genesis 1-2, God set humanity in place with specific purposes. At the fall, this plan was subverted. Humanity rebelled against God, and all creation bore the consequences. With Israel, hope dawned. All had not been lost. The story had not yet reached its end. A new chapter began.

Apart from the biblical narrative, Christians have struggled with what to make of Israel. The confusion has led to responses in the church ranging from a sense of Israeli nationalism all the way to anti-Semitism. But Israel's true significance lies within God's story where they were called to REPRESENT HUMANITY by living faithfully before God and to REDEEM HUMANITY as a witness to the nations (Deut. 4:6).

Blessing. This representative and redemptive purpose began with God's promise to a man named Abram: "I will bless you and make your name great, so that you will be a blessing. I will bless those who bless you, and him who dishonors you I will curse, and in you all the families of the earth shall be blessed" (Gen. 12:2-3). After subsequent episodes of worldwide destruction and incorrigible rebellion (Gen. 6-11), the promise to Abram was a sign that God's original plan for humanity's blessing was not lost forever. God's redemptive mission began as a particular man was chosen to partner in restoration.

Making God Known. The story continued and developed many generations later following God's deliverance of Abraham's descendants from slavery in Egypt. God's purpose for Israel was further revealed: "Now therefore, if you will indeed obey my voice and keep my covenant, you shall be my treasured possession among all peoples, for all the earth is mine; and you shall be to me a kingdom of priests and a holy nation" (Ex. 19:5-6). As a kingdom of priests, Israel was to make God known to the surrounding nations that desperately lacked the knowledge of God. They would exemplify the testimony of God's sovereign deliverance and model genuine humanity in their obedience to God. In this way, Israel would be a witness to the surrounding nations (Deut. 4:6). Through Israel's national priesthood, Abraham's blessing to the nations would be realized.

Reigning. Later still, the final aspect of God's purpose for humanity was reintroduced through Israel's narrative: cooperative participation in God's reign. This promise came to Israel's kingly archetype, David: "And your house and your kingdom shall be made sure forever before me. Your throne shall be established forever" (2 Sam. 7:16). Once again, God had not given up on his creative intentions for humanity. He set people in place in the garden to govern creation on his behalf. And now, through the faithful reign of David and his descendants, Israel was to be a witness to the surrounding nations of God's restored purpose for humanity.

Nuances. However, each renewed aspect of humanity's purpose in God came through Israel with its own nuance as the story progressed from Creation to Israel.

- The blessing was now conditional & associated with a potential curse (Leviticus 26).

- The knowledge of God could come through both deliverance from evil & oppression and through judgment of sin & rebellion (Deuteronomy 29).

- The throne of David was only established as the people rejected God as their king (1 Sam. 8:7).

Though Israel's narrative reverberates with many of the same features as Creation, a great deal had changed. Creation had spiraled into decay and futility after the fall. Even so, God's story was progressing:

Israel was set apart as a particular people to represent genuine humanity in the midst of a fallen world and also to be a redemptive witness among the nations through whom the blessing, knowledge, and reign of God would once again proliferate through Creation.

Israel's chapter, however, was not to be the final chapter in redemption. Despite their high calling, Israel was plagued with the same rebellion that defined the rest of humanity. Ironically, as Israel fell prey to self-obsession as a chosen people, they became more and more like the surrounding nations. Like the rest of humanity, they rebelled against God's purpose and dominion. So like Egypt and many nations before them, Israel came to know God through the judgment of their sin. In a scene reminiscent of the Fall (Genesis 3), Israel's Old Testament narrative grinds to a halt with the people once again exiled from their home and from the presence of their God.

Son of David. We know by now that Jesus wasn't a random act of divine intervention. He's where all of God's story came together and turned toward ultimate restoration and renewal. As we discovered last week, Jesus redeemed and fulfilled God's purposes for humanity that were established at Creation. He also fulfilled God's calling for Israel that emerge throughout the Old Testament:

- Through Jesus, God's promise to Abraham is fulfilled and all the world is blessed.

- Through Jesus, God's covenant with Moses and Israel is fulfilled. God is made known, and the royal priesthood reaches its culmination.

- Through Jesus, David's throne is eternally established – not just over Israel, but over all Creation.

A powerful reminder...

As was initially the case for humanity at large, Israel forgot their larger context. Though they clung to God's promises, they also grew victim to self-interest. They sought God's blessing...for themselves. They sought the knowledge of God...for themselves. And they sought dominion and authority...for themselves. But when Jesus arrived on the scene, most of Israel was blinded by its own self-centeredness.

This must not be the case for us as Jesus' followers today. We must remember the story in which we find ourselves. We must resist the same temptation toward self-interest that is left unchallenged when Jesus is reduced to a "personal Savior," a means of "individual forgiveness," and an opportunity for "personal relationship with God."

Reimagining Discipleship

We must not place ourselves at the center of God's story. We can never lose sight of Jesus. Our Redeemer. Our King.

Instead, we should rejoice that God invites us to be part of something so much bigger than ourselves. We must embrace his invitation to live beyond our own interests and to take our places as faithful servants within his eternal Kingdom. We must be reminders to the world of what it means to be truly human: to be blessed and to be a blessing, to know God and make him known, and to submit to and someday participate in his reign over all creation.

RETHINKING & RESPONDING

Day #1: In your own words, describe Israel's role in God's story:

_____

_____

_____

_____

_____

Describe the significance of Jesus' Israelite heritage:

_____

_____

_____

Day #2: What lessons can you learn & apply to your own life from Israel's example as a people called into God's redemptive mission?

_____

_____

_____

_____

_____

Day #3: What practical steps could you take to counteract the temptation toward self-centeredness and self-interest that caused both humanity and Israel to be exiled from God's purposes and presence?

_____

_____

_____

_____

_____

_____

Reimagining Discipleship

DAILY PRACTICES: JESUS' WAY OF LIVING

Continue each of the following practices:

Practice #1: "Reorienting" (Bible Reading)

Practice #2: "Pages" (Prayer)

Practice #3: "Present to God" (Silence & Solitude)

Practice #4: "Present to Others" (Media/tech Abstention)

Practice #5: "Re-Sourcing" (24/36 Fasting)

Practice #6: "Psalm 23" (Memorization & Meditation)

CONNECT

Over the coming week, how can we support, encourage, celebrate, and pray for each other?

_____

_____

_____

_____

_____

_____

CLOSING PRAYER

Remembering.

Anticipating.

Participating.

ISRAEL: Notes & Reflections

_____

_____

_____

_____

_____

_____

WEEK 7 - THE SON OF GOD

OPENING PRAYER:
Remembering.
Anticipating.
Participating.

FOLLOW-UP

How did God speak to you over the past week?

_____

_____

_____

How were you able cooperate with God's work in someone around you?

_____

_____

_____

_____

What were the successes & challenges of your daily practices?

_____

_____

_____

_____

How has meditation on Psalm 23 reshaped your perspective and experience of daily circumstances?

_____

_____

_____

"GOD"

Over the past two weeks, we examined how Jesus fulfilled both God's purposes for humanity and his redemptive calling for Israel. This week, we'll add the aspect of Jesus' Messianic identity that was nearly impossible to anticipate – "Son of God."

As we move forward, let's not forget how audacious (and seemingly blasphemous) this claim really was – and still is! Every Jew would have been familiar with the legendary feats of Moses: the plagues leading to Israel's freedom from Egypt, the Red Sea parting for Israel and then collapsing on the Egyptian army, the manna sustaining millions of people wandering through the wilderness, the river of water flowing out of a rock. Moses was the man! And how about Elijah? He initiated and then ended a 3.5 year draught; he raised people from the dead. And when Elijah's time came, he didn't die! He just ascended to heaven right in front of his protege.

Yet no one was foolish enough to call either of these men God.

So what made things different with Jesus? Of course, we know NOW that Jesus was the Son of God, but how and why did the first disciples reach that conclusion? Our search for an answer, once again, drives us into the story. Jesus didn't appear out of nowhere. A lot had already unfolded when he arrived on the scene. With humanity. With Israel. And with God.

God in Creation. Obviously, God had great intentions for Creation. Humanity was the centerpiece within Creation, but we were not left here alone to fend for ourselves. We were created to govern Creation on behalf of God...while being like God and reflecting him into all Creation...while walking with God and knowing him quite well. In this initial scenario, CREATION was God's resting place (Genesis. 2:2). Not a temple. Not a sanctuary. A whole Creation – the heavens and the earth together in all of God's creative glory.

This beautiful scene was ravaged in the rebellion. And as a result, HUMANITY WAS EXILED – from God's presence & purpose and from their God-given niche in Creation known as the Garden of Eden.

God in Israel. Several generations later, God called Abraham and his descendants (Israel) both as faithful representatives of humanity and as a redemptive witness among the nations. To fulfill this universal and redemptive mission, God set apart a special people within a special land.

Beyond their calling, another significant part of what made Israel so unique among the nations was that they were the caretakers of God's Temple. Although humanity at large had been exiled from God's presence in the rebellion, Israel's Temple now stood as a reminder of what once was. It was filled with imagery from Creation. And it was the one place on earth where the lines still blurred between the heavens and the earth. Although it was only accessible to the high priest one day each year, God was still present within Creation in the inner-most sanctuary of the Temple.

As we know, Israel fell to sin and rebellion. Rather than being a light to the world, Israel succumbed to idolatry and self-interest. As a result, ISRAEL WAS EXILED – from God's presence and from their God-given land and purpose. Ten tribes were overtaken and assimilated into the Assyrian Empire around 722 B.C. A little more than a century later in 586 B.C., the remaining tribes were conquered and exiled into Babylon. In the midst of Israel's fall to sin and corruption, the prophet Ezekiel witnessed the presence of God withdrawing from the Temple and ascending back into the heavens before the Temple's ultimate destruction in the Babylonian invasion (Ezekiel 10).

Prophetic Hope. Yet amidst Israel's failure and subsequent exile, a prophetic hope began echoing... Exile would come to an end. Rebellion & sin would be forgiven. And on the heels of forgiveness, God's presence would return. The Kingdom would be reestablished according to the lineage of David. This restoration would be possible because of a coming transformation:

And I will give them one heart, and a new spirit I will put within them. I will remove the heart of stone from their flesh and give them a heart of flesh that they may walk in my statutes and keep my rules and obey them. And they shall be my people, and I will be their God (Ezekiel 11:19-20).

Where humanity had repeatedly failed, GOD PROMISED TO
INTERVENE and accomplish for humanity what they could not
accomplish for themselves.

So amidst fiery judgments on Israel's sin, this prophetic hope
continued to echo:
  • Israel would live into their purposes before and on behalf of
     humanity.
  • All humanity would once again glorify God.
  • All creation would be restored.

The prophets insisted that God's plans would not be thwarted forever.
He would intervene where humanity had failed: Sin would be forgiven.
Exile would end. God's presence would return. His purposes would be
fulfilled. The Old Testament ends in the poignant juxtaposition of this
prophetic hope amidst catastrophic failure.

Son of God. Though we now have the benefit of hindsight, it was very
difficult for Israel to anticipate the means by which God would
accomplish all that had been foretold. In fact, in the days of the New
Testament, much of Israel had grown dull to the hope and purposes of
God. Many others had taken things into their own hands. And when
God's plan finally took shape in Jesus Christ, they failed to recognize
God's invention – the dawning of their own redemption.

But the mystery and wonder of Jesus was not lost on everyone. The
earliest disciples of Jesus realized what was happening. They knew
God's story. They knew the Old Testament prophetic hope. And after
centuries of divine silence, they recognized the unthinkable – God's
intervention had come to pass in and through Jesus...the Son of God!

Forgiveness.

The end of exile.

The return of God's presence.

The renewal of God's people.

RETHINKING & RESPONDING

Day #1: In your own words, describe Israel's prophetic expectations of divine intervention that were fulfilled in Jesus Christ:

_____

_____

_____

_____

In the context of God's story, describe the significance & implications of the forgiveness of sin:

_____

_____

_____

Day #2: What areas in your life look bleak or hopeless and need divine intervention? What might redemption look like in these areas?

_____

_____

_____

_____

Day #3: How can you embrace God's intervention through Jesus Christ in your own life? (Forgiveness. God's presence. Restored purpose. A new heart capable of faithfulness & obedience.)

_____

_____

_____

_____

_____

_____

Reimagining Discipleship

DAILY PRACTICES: JESUS' WAY OF LIVING

Practice #1: "Reorienting" (Bible Reading)
Practice #2: "Pages" (Prayer)
Practice #3: "Present to God" (Silence & Solitude)
Practice #4: "Present to Others" (Media/tech Abstention)
Practice #5: "Re-Sourcing" (24/36 Fasting)
Practice #6: "Psalm 23" (Memorization & Meditation)

CONNECT
Over the coming week, how can we support, encourage, celebrate, and pray for each other?

_____

_____

_____

_____

_____

_____

CLOSING PRAYER
Remembering.
Anticipating.
Participating.

GOD: Notes & Reflections

_____

_____

_____

_____

_____

_____

_____

WEEK 8 - THE MESSIAH

OPENING PRAYER:
Remembering.
Anticipating.
Participating.

FOLLOW-UP

How has your understanding & appreciation of Jesus grown over the past three weeks?

_____

_____

_____

_____

What were your successes & challenges in your daily practices over the past week?

_____

_____

_____

What practices are you finding most conducive for hearing God speak and tuning in to God's work in and around you?

_____

_____

_____

Were you able to hold Psalm 23 in your thoughts over the past week and gain new perspective as you went through the week's circumstances?

_____

_____

_____

Reimagining Discipleship

"THE MESSIAH"

At this point, we have come far enough to appreciate the greatest man born to a woman before Jesus' arrival – John the Baptist (Matthew 11:11). With some thoughtful reflection on his ministry in the context of all that we have learned together, we can now appreciate the explosive anticipation garnered by the forerunner of the Messiah.

Imagine this scenario...
A wild and controversial prophet emerges after centuries of divine silence. He's inviting Israel out into the wilderness to re-enter God's promised land through the Jordan river in a prophetic act of baptism for repentance from sin. And as he does so, he's announcing some good news: The Kingdom of God is within reach! And there was someone among them who would immerse the people in the presence of God!

Imagine the ancient memories and hope that John the Baptist was awakening in the people. John was acting out & proclaiming the imminent fulfillment of the deepest longings and hopes of Israel!

"The time has finally come! Our exile is ended! The Kingdom is at hand! God is returning!"

This explosive anticipation was the context into which Jesus stepped and began his ministry. The mysterious and long prophesied Messiah – a seemingly irreconcilable vision of Israel's King, the prophet Isaiah's "suffering servant" (Isaiah 53), the promised "prophet like Moses" (Deuteronomy 18), the Redeemer, the Son of Man, the Son of David, the Son of God – had come. Beyond anyone's wildest expectations, this was all to be fulfilled in and through one man – Jesus...the Christ.

Let's place all this within the context of God's story:

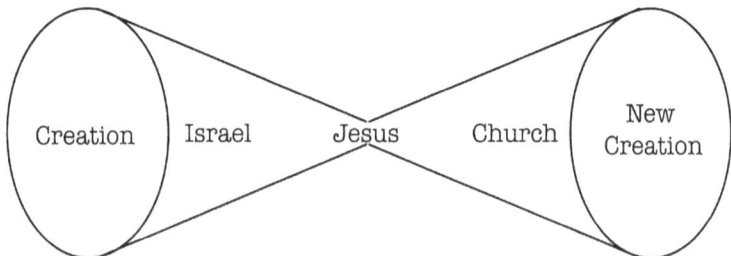

Creation Israel Jesus Church New Creation

As the center and apex of God's story, everything sovereignly pointed toward the coming of Jesus Christ, in whom all things are fulfilled and on whom the story turns. The full wreckage of humanity collapsed onto the cross in all its fury. Evil, rebellion, sin, and death culminated in the crucifixion of perfect love. But in the face of what looked like ultimate disaster, the fullness of sin and death was absorbed at the cross and then epically defeated at Jesus' resurrection. The renewal which all creation now anticipates became a reality in Jesus' resurrection (Rom. 8:22). The story turned.

Bigger Jesus. In light of God's epic victory in and through Jesus Christ, perhaps it is no wonder that the phrase "personal Savior" never appears in the Bible. In fact, the New Testament shows very little concern for individual forgiveness or passage to heaven upon death. You and I were never intended to be the center of the story. God is not concerned with us escaping from creation.

The gospel just isn't big enough or good enough when individual forgiveness, security, and well being after death are its center. Instead, Jesus is the center. He's where everything comes together. And he's MUCH bigger than most people realize:

Jesus is **the quintessential human**.

Jesus is **the faithful Israelite**.

Jesus is **God incarnate**.

Jesus is **the Messiah**.

What was accomplished in and through him is FAR greater than most people ever imagine. And we're being swept into this same story! We're invited to share in his victory! We're invited to take part in something much bigger than ourselves. We're offered a place in a coming, eternal Kingdom – Jesus' reign over the New Creation.

Reimagining Discipleship

RETHINKING & RESPONDING

Day #1: How is Jesus bigger than you used to realize?

_____

_____

_____

How does Jesus as "personal Savior" impact you differently than Jesus
the Messiah - Redeemer and King of all Creation, Son of Man, Son of
David, Son of God?

_____

_____

_____

Day #2: Are there areas in your life where it is hard to make Jesus the
center? Where does Jesus need to be bigger?

_____

_____

_____

How could you begin to make Jesus more the center in those areas?

_____

_____

_____

Day #3: In your own words, describe Jesus' significance & meaning:

_____

_____

_____

_____

_____

_____

DAILY PRACTICES: JESUS' WAY OF LIVING

Practice #1: "Reorienting" (Bible Reading)
Practice #2: "Pages" (Prayer)
Practice #3: "Present to God" (Silence & Solitude)
Practice #4: "Present to Others" (Media/tech Abstention)
Practice #5: "Re-Sourcing" (24/36 Fasting)
Practice #6: "Psalm 23" (Memorization & Meditation)

CONNECT
Over the coming week, how can we support, encourage, celebrate, and pray for each other?

_____
_____
_____
_____
_____
_____

CLOSING PRAYER
Remembering.
Anticipating.
Participating.

THE MESSIAH: Notes & Reflections

_____
_____
_____
_____
_____
_____

Part 3:

What is the Church?

Reimagining Discipleship

INTRODUCTION

Church can be a confusing topic. Most people think of "Church" as the building where a particular group of people gather to engage in religious rituals. Others see "Church" as a religious non-profit organization. Many Christians hold to the idea that the "Church" is comprised of the people themselves rather than either a building or an organization. But "people" isn't much of an identity. It isn't enough for us to live by. It is too vague to grip our imaginations and shape our daily lives. Important questions still linger...

- What does it actually mean to be the Church?
- What is our aim? What is our purpose?
- Is there a difference (biblically speaking) between attending worship services and being the "Church"?
- Does membership in a local congregation make us the "Church"?

These are the questions we hope to understand over the following four weeks. To gain a clearer understanding of the Church, we turn once again to God's story. As with Jesus, "Church" becomes a much more poignant and powerful identity when considered within its proper context.

Before moving on, let's recap our overviews of God's story from Part 1. First, God's story is redemptive in nature. It's both progressive and reflexive:

A. Creation
    B. Israel
        C. Jesus Christ
    B'. Church
A'. New Creation

Additionally, the story has a specific scope and trajectory:

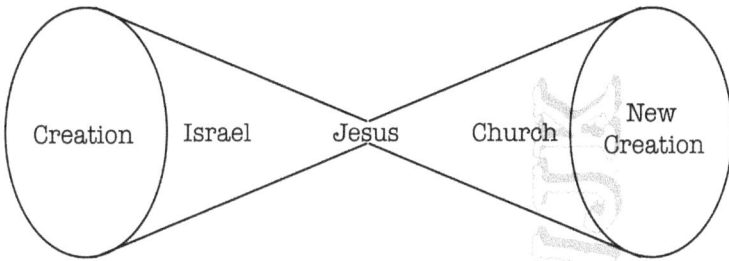

To point out the obvious, the Church is the people taking their place in God's story between Jesus and the New Creation. It is a people aligned with God's redemptive mission – living beyond themselves for the sake of others in anticipation of their cooperative participation in Jesus' reign over the New Creation.

WEEK 9 - THE STORIED CHURCH

<u>OPENING PRAYER:</u>
Remembering (what God has done).
Anticipating (what God has yet to do).
Participating (in his ongoing work in and around us).

<u>FOLLOW-UP</u>

What have been your highlights from the past 8 weeks together?

1. _____

2. _____

3. _____

What are your take-aways from "Who is Jesus?"

1. _____

2. _____

3. _____

What practices are you finding to be the most helpful in creating space for God to speak to you and to work in your life?

1. _____

2. _____

3. _____

Are there any other disciplines/practices you've observed in your reading that you think you'd like to try? How?

_____

_____

_____

_____

_____

_____

What is the Church?

This week, we'll consider the Church within the context of God's story. Despite the confusion about what Church is and isn't, God has actually revealed the nature and mission of the Church quite clearly within the scriptures. And it's "Church" from God's perspective that we're most concerned with.

So what do we know about Church?

The Church is a particular people taking their place in God's story between Jesus and the New Creation. We undertake our roles in anticipation of the King's return even as the New Creation is birthed within us as we begin new life in Jesus (2 Corinthians 5:17):

- The Church is a people of VISION: We are shaped by memory and anticipation. We know where our story began and we know where it's heading. And we're living accordingly – as witnesses to the world of what it means to be TRULY HUMAN (according to God's creative design).

- The Church is a people of ACTION: We are a people engaged in God's redemptive mission. We understand God's creative intentions for both humanity and creation. We know how it got off track. We're understanding more and more how the story turned from catastrophe to redemption in and through Jesus. So like Jesus, we're taking our places within God's story as a people living beyond ourselves. We are cooperative participants in Jesus' continuing ministry of restoration & redemption even as we await its culmination at his return.

- The Church is a people of IDENTITY: We are fixing our eyes on Jesus – the Founder of our faith and the perfect Example of the lives we're now learning to live (Hebrews 12). We are the Body of Christ in the world today. We are learning to live according to our namesake as "Christ"ians. We are modern day disciples – Jesus' apprentices.

Biblically speaking, the Church is also the echo and culmination of God's purposes for Israel that were realized and fulfilled in Jesus Christ. Yet our context in God's story is very different from Israel. We are a people following the life and ministry of Jesus. Because of him, we are a forgiven, renewed, spirit-filled, and empowered people going about our King's business:

- **Blessing.** The Church is a unique witness in the world because we are a blessed people – the continuing fulfillment of God's promise to Abraham. We live at peace with each other because we rest in God's blessing. We are a generous people because we trust in God's blessing. And as we have been blessed, we also live beyond ourselves as a blessing to others.

- **Knowing God.** We are also a people increasingly coming to know God. We increasingly understand who he is and who we are in him. And through the testimony of our lives – both our words and actions – we are making God known to the world around us.

- **Reigning.** In a world defined by self-interest, the Church is set apart as a people gratefully submitted to and embracing the reign of Jesus Christ over our lives. We are witnesses to the truth that Jesus is already the King – even though we don't yet see the full manifestation of his rule and authority. We remember that we were created to govern God's creation (Genesis 1-2) and we anticipate the day when we will reign with Jesus Christ over the New Creation (Revelation 22:5).

Whatever our relationship to various local organizations, gatherings, and/or buildings, our priority is to live as the Church:

- To live as a people of vision.
- To be a people of action.
- To know our identity.
- To rest in God's blessing and be a blessing to those around us.
- To increasingly know God and make him known.
- To submit to the reign of Jesus Christ over every aspect of our lives and to go about the King's business, knowing that our lives here & now will ultimately determine our places in Jesus' coming Kingdom (Luke 19).

RETHINKING & RESPONDING

Day #1: Describe God's blessing in your life. Are you able to rest in this blessing? Why or why not?

_____

_____

_____

What steps could you take to increasingly live beyond yourself to be a blessing to the world around you?

_____

_____

_____

Day #2: How are you coming to know God more?

_____

_____

Who has God brought into your life that needs to know him? How will you go about making God known to that person/s?

_____

_____

_____

Day #3: What areas of your life remain difficult to submit to the reign of Jesus?

_____

_____

How does the knowledge that you may one day reign over the New Creation with Jesus Christ impact you here & now?

_____

_____

_____

Reimagining Discipleship

Practice #1: "Reorienting" (Bible Reading)
Practice #2: "Pages" (Prayer)
Practice #3: "Present to God" (Silence & Solitude)
Practice #4: "Present to Others" (Media/tech Abstention)
Practice #5: "Re-Sourcing" (24/36 Fasting)

Throughout "What is the Church?", we have a new passage for memorization and mediation:
Practice #6: "1 Corinthians 13:4-8a" (Memorization & Meditation)

CONNECT
Over the coming week, how can we support, encourage, celebrate, and pray for each other?

_____

_____

_____

_____

_____

_____

CLOSING PRAYER
Remembering.
Anticipating.
Participating.

STORIED CHURCH: Notes & Reflections

_____

_____

_____

_____

_____

WEEK 10 - The GREAT Church

<u>OPENING PRAYER</u>:
Remembering.
Anticipating.
Participating.

<u>FOLLOW-UP</u>
How is your memorization of 1 Cor. 13:4-8a going? (If anyone has it memorized, please recite it for the group. Either this week or in the weeks to come, each person should have the opportunity to recite the passage to the group.)

How did 1 Cor. 13:4-8a impact your encounters with others this week?
_____
_____
_____

How did your practices go this week? Breakthroughs? Challenges?
_____
_____
_____

How were you able to be a blessing to others?
_____
_____

How were you able to make God known?
_____
_____

How were you able to submit yourself to the reign of Jesus Christ?
_____
_____
_____

Reimagining Discipleship

"The GREAT Church"

God's story provides great perspective as to what the Church is and isn't. From that starting point, we are well positioned to invest the next three weeks deepening our understanding of the Church through some teachings of the New Testament.

We begin our journey into the New Testament's vision of Church with a look at two pivotal scriptures commonly referred to as the Great Commission and the Great Commandment. Each passage helps further clarify our purpose & identity as the Church.

We begin with the Great Commission:

All authority in heaven and on earth has been given to me. Go therefore and make disciples of all nations, baptizing them in the name of the Father and of the Son and of the Holy Spirit, teaching them to observe all that I have commanded you. And behold, I am with you always, to the end of the age.
— Jesus Christ (Matthew 28:18-20)

Obviously, the Great Commission is contextualized within God's story. It opens with words we should now be in a good position to appreciate: "All authority in heaven and on earth has been given to [Jesus]."

- Why does Jesus have all authority? Because he is the King.

- How does this authority extend across heaven and earth? Because in and through Jesus, ALL Creation is headed toward wholeness and renewal.

As we continue into this passage, a defining attribute of the Church emerges – discipleship. While commonly understood in the 1st century, this term has lost its meaning for many people today. To help recover its original meaning, it may help us to envision something of a modern-day equivalent: apprenticeship.

An apprentice is learning to become just like the master. To think like the master. To act like the master. To do what the master does in the manner he/she does it. This is precisely Jesus' invitation and practice with his first followers. They watched & learned from the master and were then sent out to proclaim his message and continue his ministry (Luke 9-10). This is the pattern they learned from Jesus and continued in the early church. This should still be the pattern of life & ministry in the Church today:

- Be a disciple.
- Make a disciple.

The pattern is clear throughout the New Testament. And it's spelled out in the Great Commission: Make disciples everywhere you go. Immerse people in the reality of the presence of God. Teach them to obey everything Jesus taught. In short, learn to be just like Jesus and teach others to be just like Jesus.

Fans vs. Disciples

Unfortunately, many Christians today have a hard time discerning between the multitudes and the disciples. In Jesus' day (as in ours), thousands of people admired Jesus. They adored him. They appreciated him. Thousands wanted his blessing. Thousands believed that he could heal and restore them. These adoring fans comprised the "multitudes" and "great crowds" that surrounded Jesus in the New Testament. But there weren't many disciples.

Sanctuaries are often filled with such fans of Jesus today. They adore Jesus. They admire him. They want Jesus in their lives. But like the multitudes, they want him at their own discretion & on their own terms. They haven't embraced the call to apprenticeship. They're not disciples.

A silly example. Let's clarify the difference further with a contemporary example: Imagine you're sitting at a Broncos game and Peyton Manning walks over during a time out. "I've been watching you over here. I'd love for you to be my biggest fan." Broncos fan or not, that would be a pretty cool offer. It would be exciting to be personally recognized by one of the greatest quarterbacks ever. Personally, I'd probably head straight to the store after the game and buy my first

Manning jersey before calling most of my friends to tell them about what had happened.

But how much different would this be?

You're at the same game. Peyton Manning walks over during a time out: "Hey you. Come down here. I've been watching you. I want you to be my apprentice. I'm going to teach you everything I know about football. I'm going to teach you to do everything I do as well as I've ever done it. I want you to become a quarterback just like me."

This second offer – apprenticeship – is entirely different. It would be exciting to be Peyton Manning's greatest fan and to be acknowledged by him. It would be a great story to tell your friends. But to become his apprentice would be a life changer. Life would never be the same. Before the whole (football) world, you would become a new person – Peyton Manning's apprentice.

There's a big difference between a fan and an apprentice. Jesus never asked for fans. He made & commissioned disciples. As his Church, this pattern is ours to continue today. Everywhere we go:

- Being disciples.
- Making disciples.
- Immersing ourselves in the reality of the presence of God.
- Obeying everything Jesus taught.

In this way, we might carry on our legacy as the Church. We could say with Paul and those that have gone before us:

"Be imitators of me, as I am of Christ"
(1 Corinthians 11:1)

"Whatever you have learned and received and heard and seen in me – practice these things."
(Philippians 4:9)

As we go about fulfilling Jesus' Great Commission, we set ourselves apart as the Church. Now let's add the second GREAT – The Great Commandment:

> You shall love the Lord your God with all your heart and with all your soul and with all your mind. This is the great and first commandment. And a second is like it: You shall love your neighbor as yourself.
> —Jesus (Matthew 22:37-39)

There's a common misperception among Christians that our knowledge, beliefs, and morality define us and set us apart from the world. But from Jesus' perspective, we are defined by love. He says that when we love well, we fulfill all of God's purposes for us (Matthew 22:40). So what does it mean to be the Church? It means we love well. This warrants a deeper look at the biblical notion of love.

While the contemporary notion of love is a sentiment that people "fall" in and out of, biblical love is life-shaping. It's intentional. It's active. It's costly.

For example, let's take 1 Corinthians 13 (our Memory/Meditation passage):

> Love is patient and kind; love does not envy or boast; it is not arrogant or rude. It does not insist on its own way; it is not irritable or resentful; it does not rejoice at wrongdoing, but rejoices with the truth. Love bears all things, believes all things, hopes all things, endures all things. Love never fails. (1 Corinthians 13:4-8a)

This passage makes for a cute little reading when everyone is dressed up at a charming wedding ceremony. But it's gritty and challenging in a marriage (and in any real relationship). Patient? Kind? Doesn't insist on having its own way? Not irritable or resentful? Bears all things? This is not the "love" we hear about in pop culture and mass media. This is not an emotion. This is commitment. This is hard work. This is costly. This is a love that should define the Church and set us apart from the rest of the world as a very unique people.

As we conclude the GREAT Church, let's turn to one more verse in which Jesus pulls everything together:

> A new commandment I give to you, that you love one another: just as I have loved you, you also are to love one another. By this all people will know that you are my disciples, if you have love for one another."
> —Jesus (John 13:34)

Long story short – we're to be like Jesus. And preeminently so in love:

- In loving well, we are a blessing.
- In loving well, we make God known.
- In loving well, we submit ourselves to Jesus' example and purpose.
- In loving well, we reveal ourselves to be Jesus' disciples.
- In loving well, we are the Church.

RETHINKING & RESPONDING

Day #1: In your own words, describe what it means to be a disciple:

_____

_____

_____

Describe the characteristics that make the Church GREAT:

_____

_____

_____

Day #2: How is God speaking to YOU about what it means for YOU to be the Church?

_____

_____

_____

Day #3: How/where do you need to grow as an apprentice of Jesus Christ? How will you go about the process?

_____

_____

_____

_____

Who in your life is God stirring you to love better? Who can you talk to about this for support and encouragement?

_____

_____

_____

_____

Reimagining Discipleship

<u>DAILY PRACTICES: JESUS' WAY OF LIVING</u>

Practice #1: "Reorienting" (Bible Reading)
Practice #2: "Pages" (Prayer)
Practice #3: "Present to God" (Silence & Solitude)
Practice #4: "Present to Others" (Media/tech Abstention)
Practice #5: "Re-Sourcing" (24/36 Fasting)
Practice #6: "1 Corinthians 13:4-8a" (Memorization & Meditation)

<u>CONNECT</u>
Over the coming week, how can we support, encourage, celebrate, and pray for each other?

_____

_____

_____

_____

_____

_____

<u>CLOSING PRAYER</u>
Remembering.
Anticipating.
Participating.

<u>The GREAT Church: Notes & Reflections</u>

_____

_____

_____

_____

_____

_____

_____

WEEK 11 - THE BODY OF CHRIST

<u>OPENING PRAYER</u>:
Remembering.
Anticipating.
Participating.

<u>FOLLOW-UP</u>

How is God working in you?

_____

_____

_____

_____

How are you cooperating with what God's doing?

_____

_____

_____

_____

What were your successes & challenges loving others this week?

_____

_____

_____

How did your identity as a disciple affect your decision making this week?

_____

_____

_____

_____

"THE BODY OF CHRIST"

We began answering the question "What is the Church?" from the broad perspective of God's story and specifically how the Church emerges within it. This broad view provided a foundation upon which we could build with specific New Testament passages.

The first two New Testament passages to which we turned were the GREATs: the Great Commission (Matthew 28) and the Great Commandment (Matthew 22).

This week, we return to the New Testament to consider three more passages that each point toward a common aspect of being the Church:

We can only be the Church TOGETHER.

1 Corinthians 12:1-31. (Read it.) People have always been people. And people have always made up the Church. While there is a temptation to romanticize the New Testament church, there is ample evidence that the first generation of the Church struggled with many of the same issues that churches struggle with today.

In the case of the first century Corinthian church, Paul wrote multiple letters addressing some familiar issues: sexual perversion/immorality, self-promotion, and disunity. His response to the latter issues comes together nicely in 1 Corinthians 12 and provides us with a powerful metaphor for the Church.

Paul begins by acknowledging something easily recognized but difficult to reconcile: God has gifted and empowered us all differently. From the 1st to the 21st century, this beautiful diversity has tested the character of God's people because we are constantly surrounded with people to whom God has given gifts and abilities that we don't have ourselves.

Amidst jealousy and segregation in the Corinthian church concerning this diversity, Paul wrote to his brothers and sisters to remind them that their uniqueness was by God's design and for their common good. This line of thought led Paul to a famous metaphor for the Church:

For just as the body is one and has many members, and all the members of the body, though many, are one body, so it is with Christ (1 Cor. 12:12).

As Paul continues over the remainder of chapter 12, he drives home these truths about the Church:

- As the Body of Christ, our unique members complement one another. God didn't design us as autonomous, independent beings. We need each other so that we can more effectively be who God created us to be and accomplish what God created us to accomplish.

- We are only whole when we are together. We can only fully participate with God's work in and around us when we're working alongside one another.

Romans 12:3-8. (Read it.) The Corinthians weren't the only New Testament Church that needed to be reminded of the beauty in the diversity of the Church. In Romans 12, Paul returns to the metaphor of the Church as the Body of Christ. The same truths from 1 Corinthians 12 are confirmed and expounded upon in Paul's letter to the Romans:

- None of us should think of ourselves too highly. We should all be humble.

- We should appreciate the fact that God is the one who gives faith and grace to all of us, regardless of our differences.

- We should all be who God has called & created us to be. And we should serve each other in the manner God has gifted us to serve.

Ephesians 4:1-16. (Read it.) In this final "Body of Christ" passage, Paul repeats many of his previous points. He also specifically addresses some of the more prominent gifts. This passage is worth noting because these often prove to be the most problematic in the church as they are most likely to incite jealousy and conflict.

Fortunately, Paul lays a very helpful foundation toward understanding how these giftings are to function. First, they are not intended to function alone. Each of these five-fold gifts are unique. They have particular inclinations. They must learn to function together in order to maximize their benefit in the Church. Second, it's not prominence or recognition that sets these giftings apart; it's the end result by which they can be identified:

- EVERYONE in the body is built up and equipped for ministry
- EVERYONE becomes increasingly like Jesus
- The WHOLE BODY grows and builds itself up in love

RETHINKING & RESPONDING

Day #1: What are some of the challenges and rewards of submitting yourself within the Church as one member of Christ's body among many others?

_____
_____
_____
_____
_____
_____

Day #2: How has God uniquely created and gifted you? And how might your uniqueness impact others in the Church for the common good?

_____
_____
_____
_____
_____
_____

Day #3: How could you plug in to your local church body and begin serving others for the common good?

_____
_____
_____
_____
_____
_____
_____

Reimagining Discipleship

Practice #1: "Reorienting" (Bible Reading)
Practice #2: "Pages" (Prayer)
Practice #3: "Present to God" (Silence & Solitude)
Practice #4: "Present to Others" (Media/tech Abstention)
Practice #5: "Re-Sourcing" (24/36 Fasting)
Practice #6: "1 Corinthians 13:4-8a" (Memorization & Meditation)

CONNECT
Over the coming week, how can we support, encourage, celebrate, and pray for each other?

_____

_____

_____

_____

_____

_____

CLOSING PRAYER
Remembering.
Anticipating.
Participating.

THE BODY OF CHRIST: Notes & Reflections

_____

_____

_____

_____

_____

_____

WEEK 12 - HEIRS

<u>OPENING PRAYER</u>:
Remembering.
Anticipating.
Participating.

<u>FOLLOW-UP</u>

How has the memory passage come up and impacted your actions toward others over the past week?

_____

_____

_____

How are your practices creating space for God to speak and work in & around you?

_____

_____

_____

In what areas are you hoping for breakthrough and growth in becoming more like Jesus Christ?

_____

_____

_____

What opportunities did you have to cooperate with others in being the Church? To be a blessing? To make God known? To mutually submit yourselves to Jesus?

_____

_____

_____

Reimagining Discipleship

"HEIRS"

For our final topic in "What is the Church?", we're going to trace two related concepts that run throughout the New Testament. As with most topics in "When Jesus is King," these concepts will likely be familiar to those who have been part of a local congregation for a while. But it's also likely that they've never been taken too seriously.

Our final addition to "What is the Church?":

- The Church is a co-HEIR with Jesus Christ of the New Creation. The New Creation is our INHERITANCE in the Lord (Romans 8; Galatians 4; Ephesians 1; Titus 3).

- When God's Kingdom culminates at Jesus' return, we'll be set in place to REIGN over it (2 Timothy 2; Revelation 5 & 22).

Imagine with me for a moment that you have the greatest, most compassionate, most brilliant uncle ever. From the day you were born, he's been watching over you – thrilled with every step you've taken and with every aspect of your development. Although he's very modest and humble, this uncle happens to be the owner, president, and CEO of a multibillion-dollar company. And from the day you were born, he's been grooming you and inviting you into his business that you might share in it with him. You are his heir. You are his apprentice.

How would life be different if it was shaped by such anticipation and knowledge? What hard decisions would you be free to make knowing this was your future? What various circumstances would you now be empowered to endure as the heir to your uncle's kingdom?

What if this scenario were true, except the reality was infinitely bigger? What if the Kingdom encompassed ALL of creation? What if you'd step into this inheritance for ETERNITY?

How would life be different...here? Now?

"...No longer will there be anything accursed, but the throne of God and of the Lamb will be in (the city), and his servants will worship him. They will see his face, and his name will be on their foreheads. And night will be no more. They will need no light of lamp or sun, for the Lord God will be their light, and THEY will reign forever and ever" (Revelation 22:3-5).

This is the future for the Church. This is the anticipation of all those who live in faithful service of Jesus Christ. Though this scenario seems surreal, it is much easier to grasp with the whole biblical narrative in mind. God created humanity to govern creation on his behalf. Despite the initial catastrophe, Jesus put creation back on course. God's plans will not be thwarted. Creation will be renewed and restored and God's people will reign over the New Creation under Jesus Christ.

Romans 8:11-17. (Read it.) At this point, our understanding of discipleship should be growing even deeper. Following Jesus and submitting ourselves to a life of discipleship is not some religious act. It is the reasonable response once we understand what's really unfolding around us. If we believe that things are coming to pass as indicated in the scriptures, embracing discipleship wholeheartedly and with great effort only makes sense.

As with everything in life worth doing, however, discipleship comes at a cost. This inheritance comes at a cost. We must lay aside our own ambitions and desires to be adopted into God's family and to inherit the Kingdom. If we cling to our lives, we'll lose them; but if we "lay down our lives" to live for Jesus Christ, only then do we truly find them (Mark 8:35). This was the way Jesus modeled and it is the way for his followers.

Jesus' teaching. With this scenario in mind, many of Jesus' parables and teachings that we have recently read should be gaining both clarity and significance. Jesus wasn't making quaint, moral points. He was conveying a new reality of life because he was becoming King. He used various metaphors to reveal the true context of our lives and the corresponding invitation to take part in what was unfolding in and through him.

Count the cost. Throughout the gospels (Matthew, Mark, Luke, John) Jesus often reiterated that in order to follow him, people would have to "count the cost." Christians sometimes interpret these passages as gloomy, depressing demands. They hear the message, "Give up everything you love and hold dear and live a deprived 'Christian' life. And when you die you can go to heaven."

But this is a misinterpretation. To accurately "count the cost", we must understand both the **cost** and the **reward/benefit**. We must know the story. We must know what God is up to. And then we must consider what price we would pay now to be part of his eternal kingdom. To be clear, God's promise is not death and clouds and harps and heavenly choirs. It's much better than that. It's far more audacious:

- God's promise to you is an inheritance in an eternal Kingdom.
- God's promise to you is immortality.
- God's promise to you is reigning with Jesus over the New Creation.

This is God's invitation to you in and through Jesus Christ. So now –

COUNT THE COST.

What's this invitation worth to you?

What are you going to live for?

Who will you become in God's story?

RETHINKING & RESPONDING

Day #1: How do the passages referenced this week challenge & expand your typical thoughts about what it means to be the Church?

_____

_____

_____

_____

_____

Day #2: How is this future relevant to your life here & now?

_____

_____

_____

_____

How might God be working in and through your present circumstances to prepare you for service in his kingdom in the future?

_____

_____

_____

_____

Day #3: What adjustments/changes in your life would be appropriate and wise based on God's desired future for you in Jesus Christ?

_____

_____

_____

_____

_____

_____

Reimagining Discipleship

Practice #1: "Reorienting" (Bible Reading)
Practice #2: "Pages" (Prayer)
Practice #3: "Present to God" (Silence & Solitude)
Practice #4: "Present to Others" (Media/tech Abstention)
Practice #5: "Re-Sourcing" (24/36 Fasting)
Practice #6: "1 Corinthians 13:4-8a" (Memorization & Meditation)

CONNECT
Over the coming week, how can we support, encourage, celebrate, and
pray for each other?

_____

_____

_____

_____

_____

_____

CLOSING PRAYER
Remembering.
Anticipating.
Participating.

HEIRS: Notes & Reflections

_____

_____

_____

_____

_____

_____

Part 4:

What Now?

Reimagining Discipleship

INTRODUCTION

Our journey together began some time ago now. We started with a very broad examination of the biblical narrative as we answered the question, "What's the Story?" Along the way, we began embracing some of the life-shaping habits and disciplines Jesus modeled and taught his first disciples: engaging the scriptures, prayer, being present to God and others, and fasting.

In Parts 2 & 3, we zoomed in somewhat to consider how Jesus emerged within God's story – his significance and meaning & how everything came together in him. We then turned our attention to the Church – what the Church is within the biblical narrative and some of the ways in which our lives here & now as well as our future together set us apart as a unique people in the world.

In Part 4, we'll zoom in even further to consider four distinct visions of life for those who comprise the Church. In light of everything we've learned, it should be obvious that when we give our lives to Jesus Christ, things change. A genuinely new kind of life begins (Romans 6). The New Testament has a great deal to say about this new life. So one last time, let's turn to the Bible to answer the question for those embracing new life in Jesus Christ, "What now?"

WEEK 13 - RESURRECTION LIFE

OPENING PRAYER:
Remembering (what God has done).
Anticipating (what God has yet to do).
Participating (in his ongoing work in and around us).

FOLLOW-UP
How would you describe/summarize God's work in you over the past three months?

_____

_____

_____

Describe 3 highlights of the past three months together:
1. _____
2. _____
3. _____

What have you learned about how God works in and around you?

_____

_____

_____

What have you learned about yourself?

_____

_____

_____

What are your top 3 take-aways from "What is the Church?"
1. _____
2. _____
3. _____

"RESURRECTION LIFE"

Resurrection was central in Paul's vision of new life. Nowhere is this more obvious than in two of Paul's most famous passages: Romans 6-8 and 1 Corinthians 15. These passages contain some of the most foundational and often quoted verses in the Christian faith. This week, we're turning their direction to begin answering the question, "What now?"

Romans 6-8
(Read Romans 6:1-23.) Chapter 6 begins with some thoughts on baptism. Two major ideas emerge. First, at baptism, the believer identifies with the death of Jesus Christ in order to "rise" and walk in NEWNESS OF LIFE here & now (6:4). This newness of life becomes a present and defining reality. Second, this newness of life is defined by anticipation – not of being dead in heaven – but of a coming RESURRECTION just like Jesus (6:5). This present reality – newness of life in anticipation of resurrection – constitutes Paul's vision of life in Romans 6-8.

Now let's take a moment to point out the obvious: Our bodies (in their current states) are in desperate need of a divine overhaul. But nevertheless, we – BODIES AND ALL – are destined for resurrection life in the New Creation. Although there will be transition and transformation,

the new life we have begun in Jesus Christ will never come to an end. And when we step fully into eternity, it will be a natural extension of the lives we're now living.

So when Paul says we enter "newness of life" at baptism, he wasn't kidding. What has begun will never end!

Now is our time to live accordingly. Now is the time to set our bodies (habits and rhythms of living) apart unto God in worship (6:12-19). Now is the time to establish a trajectory in our lives before Jesus that we want to carry us into eternity.

As Paul continues in 6:15-23, you can almost hear him exhorting his friends, "Don't be naive. You're doing SOMETHING with your body. You're serving SOMETHING. You're obedient to SOMEONE's desires." The only question is what? Whose?

As Christians, this is why we have "new" life. Things are not the same as they used to be. We are learning to live wisely in light of what lies ahead. We are serving God here & now with everything we've got. We're living as a people whose lives before their King will never come to an end.

(Read Romans 8:11-30) After working through some realities of resurrection life through chapter 7, Paul reiterates and expounds on resurrection as the centerpiece of his vision for new life in chapter 8:

- You're not going to stay dead. Your BODY is not going to stay dead. You will experience the same resurrection as Jesus (Romans 8:11).

- Christians do not rightfully yearn for death and heaven. We only endure death as we (along with all of Creation) await and anticipate "the redemption of our bodies" – resurrection and renewal (Romans 8:23).

- Resurrection is the hope in which we are saved in and through Jesus Christ (Romans 8:24).

1 Corinthians 15
After looking at Romans 6-8, perhaps you're thinking,

Wow. If this resurrection stuff is for real, that's some pretty good news. People should probably know about this.

Well, you'd be in good company. This is precisely what Paul thought. So let's turn to and read the most explicit "gospel" passage in the New Testament: 1 Corinthians 15:1-57. Here is Paul's brief summary of the Good News:
- Christ died for our sins IN ACCORDANCE WITH GOD'S STORY (1 Corinthians 15:3).
- Jesus was buried (body and all)(v.4).

- Jesus was resurrected (body and all) IN ACCORDANCE WITH GOD'S STORY (v.4).

- Jesus spent time with more than 500 people after his resurrection before ascending into heaven (v.5-8).

- Jesus was the first fruit of resurrection life that will one day be shared with all his people (v.20-23).

Paul understood the entirety of God's story. He recognized what had taken place in and through Jesus. He knew Jesus wasn't an aberration. He wasn't a means for people to escape from this fallen world. He was God's ultimate victory. Jesus brought redemption. He guaranteed restoration and renewal for all creation. He defeated death in his resurrection. And some day soon, his victory will be shared with all of God's people! This is the news Paul was announcing. This is Paul's vision of new life.

Let's continue on through chapter 15 for a few more takeaways:

- We're not going to slowly evolve into resurrection life. This will be no human accomplishment. Our hope does not lie in science or medicine, despite their best attempts to prolong the inevitable breakdown of our present, mortal bodies. After all, mortal "flesh and blood" cannot inherit the Kingdom of God (v.50). Our hope lies elsewhere...

- There will come a change. Our perishable bodies will put on the imperishable. Our mortal bodies will take on immortality! (v.51-53)

- Death (not just sin) will be overcome by Jesus' victory!! (v.54-57)

- Resurrection life is a present, life-shaping reality for Jesus' people. Because resurrection lies ahead, we press ahead in service of our King Jesus in the confidence that our labor is never in vain (v.58).

So what now?

Be steadfast, immovable, always abounding in the work of the Lord, knowing that in the Lord your labor is not in vain (1 Corinthians 15:58)

RETHINKING & RESPONDING

Day #1: How do you think many Christian "heroes" have been empowered for life and ministry based on the hope and anticipation of resurrection?

_____

_____

_____

_____

_____

_____

Day #2: Are you living the kind of life before Jesus that you'd like to define you for eternity? Why or why not?

_____

_____

_____

_____

_____

_____

Day #3: What life changes are you empowered to make in light of your pending immortality as a disciple of Jesus Christ?

_____

_____

How will this change begin? What steps lie before you?

_____

_____

_____

Reimagining Discipleship

DAILY PRACTICES: JESUS' WAY OF LIVING

Practice #1: "Reorienting" (Bible Reading)
Practice #2: "Pages" (Prayer)
Practice #3: "Present to God" (Silence & Solitude)
Practice #4: "Present to Others" (Media/tech Abstention)
Practice #5: "Re-Sourcing" (24/36 Fasting)

And our passage for memorizing and meditation in Part 4:
Practice #6: "Colossians 3:1-17" (Memorization & Meditation)

CONNECT
Over the coming week, how can we support, encourage, celebrate, and pray for each other?

_____

_____

_____

_____

_____

_____

CLOSING PRAYER
Remembering.
Anticipating.
Participating.

RESURRECTION LIFE: Notes & Reflections

_____

_____

_____

_____

_____

_____

WEEK 14 - BORN AGAIN

<u>OPENING PRAYER</u>:
Remembering.
Anticipating.
Participating.

<u>FOLLOW-UP</u>

How is the memorization of Col. 3:1-17 proceeding? (If anyone has it memorized, please recite it for the group. Either this week or in the weeks to come, each person should have the opportunity to recite the passage to the group.)

Has meditating on Col. 3:1-17 impacted your life this week?

_____

_____

_____

_____

Who in your life needs to hear the good news about Jesus and all that he accomplished?
1. _____
2. _____
3. _____

Who in your life needs a better vision of new life in Jesus Christ? When/how will you talk to them about it?

_____

_____

_____

_____

_____

_____

Reimagining Discipleship

"BORN AGAIN"

For many Christians, the primary vision of new life surrounds being "born again". In many congregations and some denominations, this central focus on being "born again" has created a distinct sub-culture. It is typically focused on the essential "born again" experience (often the recitation of the "sinner's prayer" and/or water baptism). Unfortunately, there's usually not much of an answer for "What now?" beyond "Be good. Die. Go to heaven." The New Testament's insistence on discipleship is often dismissed. The "born again" experience, rather than faithfulness or obedience, becomes the litmus test for who's in and who's out...of the local congregation, of Jesus' forgiveness, of heaven and hell, of God's coming wrath & judgment.

Our current focus is not to debate the merits and validity of the "born again" sub-culture. Instead, our interest is in understanding the meaning & significance of the phrase "born again" as it pertains to our current question, "What Now?" This leads us back to the New Testament where we may consider "born again" in its biblical (rather than cultural) context.

After the past 13 weeks together, we're already aware of the larger biblical context: "Born again" is a reference to the new life of Jesus' followers between his resurrection and the culmination of his kingdom in the New Creation. Obviously, whatever is be to known about being "born again" must make sense in this context.

As for its more immediate context, the phrase "born again" appears only four times in the New Testament – twice in John 3 and twice in 1 Peter 1. We'll examine all four references below and find that they have a striking contextual similarity.

John 3. The first two "born again" references are found in John 3. The main reference is one of the most quoted verses in the Bible:

"Truly, truly, I say to you, unless one is born again, he cannot see the kingdom of God."
—Jesus (John 3:3)

108

Right away, this verse rings true with the broader context of God's story. Being "born again" is not primarily about forgiveness, death, or going to heaven; it's about entering into God's kingdom. It's about entering into his reign over all creation.

As always, Jesus retains his "kingdom" focus. It was the point to most of his parables. It was the good news that he announced. The nearness of the kingdom through Jesus' life & ministry meant that everything was changing. So in John 3, when Nicodemus (the Jewish Pharisee) approached Jesus, Jesus went where he always went – to the kingdom. And to the new life appropriate for those anticipating the coming of God's kingdom. A life so different it was like being born all over again.

Now let's move forward to the end of the same chapter:

> "Whoever believes in the Son has eternal life, whoever does not obey the Son shall not see life, but the wrath of God remains on him." (John 3:36)

Ironically, this verse defies a foundational premise of the "born again" subculture: the acquisition of forgiveness through the "born again" experience guarantees someone a place before God in heaven (regardless of discipleship or obedience). But in the broader context of God's unfolding story, John 3:36 makes perfect sense: **Jesus is not just a gate-keeper for heaven;** he is the King of all creation. Kings cannot be passed by in a moment only to be subsequently admired but practically dismissed. Regardless of their goodness, kings are not ever to be taken lightly. Kings reign. Kings are to be obeyed.

So our takeaway from John 3:
Being "born again" is not something we can acquire on our own terms through a prescribed ritual or prayer. To be "born again" is not to ascertain personal forgiveness/salvation. To be "born again" is to enter a kingdom. To be "born again" is to begin a life of submission and obedience to the King.

1 Peter 1.
(Read 1 Peter 1) The only other two references in the New Testament to "born again" occur in 1 Peter 1. Similar themes reverberate that first emerged in John 3:

"...for OBEDIENCE to Jesus Christ" (1 Peter 1:2)

"he has caused us to be BORN AGAIN" (v.3)

"As OBEDIENT children..." (v.14)

"Having purified your souls by your OBEDIENCE" (v.22)

"you have been BORN AGAIN" (v.23)

Without going into all the details of 1 Peter 1, let's state the obvious conclusion:

"Born again" cannot be separated
from obedience.

So what now? Obey Jesus.

Equipped and Empowered. For too many people, the Bible is far too mysterious and confusing. At this point in our journey together, by the grace of God, the biblical narrative has come into focus. With this focus, we have become increasingly equipped and empowered to understand the scriptures – within their proper context and in accordance with the intended meaning of their original authors.

So with the backdrop of Creation & New Creation, restoration & renewal, death & resurrection, Jesus & his Church in mind, let's drink deeply of Peter's words in 1 Peter 1 and appreciate his vision of new life within the context of God's story:

"Blessed be the God and Father of our Lord Jesus
Christ. According to his great mercy, he has caused
us to be born again to a living hope through the
resurrection of Jesus Christ from the dead, to an
inheritance that is imperishable, undefiled, and
unfading, kept in heaven for you, who by God's
power are being guarded through faith for a
salvation ready to be revealed in the last time."
(1 Peter 1:3-5)

RETHINKING & RESPONDING

Day #1: Describe the significance & meaning of being "born again" based on its biblical context: God's story, John 3, and 1 Peter 1:

_____

_____

_____

_____

_____

_____

_____

Day #2: How would you explain to someone how being "born again" and obedience to Jesus actually go hand in hand?

_____

_____

_____

_____

_____

Day #3: Who in your life might be ready to become "born again"? How could you cooperatively participate in the process?

_____

_____

_____

_____

_____

_____

Reimagining Discipleship

Practice #1: "Reorienting" (Bible Reading)
Practice #2: "Pages" (Prayer)
Practice #3: "Present to God" (Silence & Solitude)
Practice #4: "Present to Others" (Media/tech Abstention)
Practice #5: "Re-Sourcing" (24/36 Fasting)
Practice #6: "Colossians 3:1-17" (Memorization & Meditation)

CONNECT
Over the coming week, how can we support, encourage, celebrate, and pray for each other?

_____

_____

_____

_____

_____

_____

CLOSING PRAYER
Remembering.
Anticipating.
Participating.

BORN AGAIN: Notes & Reflections

_____

_____

_____

_____

_____

_____

_____

WEEK 15 - ETERNAL LIFE

<u>OPENING PRAYER</u>:
Remembering.
Anticipating.
Participating.

<u>FOLLOW-UP</u>

As God continues his work in your life, what steps of obedience may lie ahead of you?

_____

_____

_____

_____

_____

How have you been able to participate in leading someone into new life in Jesus Christ?

_____

_____

_____

_____

How are your practices contributing to your transformation in Jesus Christ?

_____

_____

_____

_____

_____

Reimagining Discipleship

"ETERNAL LIFE"

Before reaching the end of our journey together through REIMAGINING DISCIPLESHIP, we'll take two more looks at the new life envisioned for us in the New Testament as Jesus' followers living in anticipation of the New Creation.

Oftentimes, the passages we read convey straightforward truth that we fail to recognize because of our preconceived ideas. This is often the case with being "born again." It also happens regarding our understanding of eternal life.

This week, we'll examine a series of Jesus' references to eternal life through the gospel of John. Here's a sneak peek at what we're about to discover:

Eternal life is a PRESENT REALITY.

Let's begin by reading the following "eternal life" references aloud to each other: John 3:15-16 & 36; 4:36; 5:24; 6:47 & 54; 10:28; 11:25.

Notice Jesus' consistent reference to eternal life as a present reality.

Let's clarify a couple things before we go any further.
1. The present reality of eternal life does not diminish its "eternal" nature. Eternal life simply begins much sooner than we may have initially thought.
2. The present reality of eternal life doesn't imply that the way things are today will be the way that they'll be forever. As we read a few weeks ago in 1 Corinthians 15, there is a forthcoming transformation. Though we're already determining our places in Jesus' kingdom by the way we're living, life will be MUCH different when the kingdom is fully manifest. Death will be swallowed up by life. Mortality will give way to immortality.

114

By now, in light of all that we've been learning about God's story, the present reality of eternal life should make sense to us. And so it should be no surprise that this same perspective is consistent throughout Jesus' teaching – particularly in his parables.

Remember one more time Jesus' parable in Luke 19: The citizens and servants defined themselves in the kingdom BEFORE the King returned. Jesus taught his disciples that **the trajectory of their lives based on their priorities and allegiance would naturally extend into his kingdom**. In other words, their everyday lives were already eternally significant. The same is true for us today.

So pulling together this week with where we've been over the past four months, let's add a few quick summary thoughts regarding eternal life:

- **Eternal life is a natural extension of the lives we are now living.** So Jesus refers to it as a present reality for those who have come to know him.
- One day, the veil will be taken away, and we'll see things more clearly, but **we'll still be us, and the reality in which we find ourselves will be the same that it's always been**.
- Though his reign is not yet fully manifest, **we are already living WHEN JESUS IS KING**. We're already defining ourselves within his reign.
- **The more we come to know & serve Jesus and to live in fellowship with him, the more we're living an eternal kind of life** (John 17:3).

So again, what now?

Let's live well. Let's be faithful to Jesus in our relationships. In our finances. In our time management. In our allegiance. Let's embrace Jesus as our Lord and King here & now. And then when the day comes and he returns to finalize his victory, we'll find ourselves quite at home as we transition into his eternal kingdom.

Reimagining Discipleship

RETHINKING & RESPONDING

Day #1: In your own words, describe how eternal life is a present reality.

_____

_____

_____

Why do you think Jesus repeatedly made this point (about the present-ness of eternity) to his followers?

_____

_____

_____

Day #2: Describe the current trajectory of your life before Jesus and how it will launch you into eternity:

_____

_____

_____

Are there changes you'd like to make in your life based on how you want to emerge into Jesus' kingdom?

_____

_____

_____

Day #3: How will you begin to adjust your life's trajectory? What partners will you need to help you succeed?

_____

_____

_____

_____

_____

DAILY PRACTICES: JESUS' WAY OF LIVING

Practice #1: "Reorienting" (Bible Reading)
Practice #2: "Pages" (Prayer)
Practice #3: "Present to God" (Silence & Solitude)
Practice #4: "Present to Others" (Media/tech Abstention)
Practice #5: "Re-Sourcing" (24/36 Fasting)
Practice #6: "Colossians 3:1-17" (Memorization & Meditation)

CONNECT
Over the coming week, how can we support, encourage, celebrate, and
pray for each other?

_____

_____

_____

_____

_____

_____

CLOSING PRAYER
Remembering.
Anticipating.
Participating.

ETERNAL LIFE: Notes & Reflections

_____

_____

_____

_____

_____

_____

WEEK 16 - TEMPLES

OPENING PRAYER:
Remembering.
Anticipating.
Participating.

FOLLOW-UP
Describe your growth as a disciple of Jesus Christ over the course of
REIMAGINING DISCIPLESHIP.

_____

_____

_____

_____

What practices have been most life-shaping? Why?

_____

_____

_____

_____

How is God leading you to continue and/or modify your discipleship
practices in the weeks/months that lie ahead? Who will be there to
support you in your continued growth?

_____

_____

_____

Who around you is God calling you to equip and empower in the
scriptures and as a disciple of Jesus Christ? How will you begin the
process with them? What are your next steps?

_____

_____

"TEMPLES"

It's hard to believe that this is our last week together! My hope and prayer is that God has done such a work in each of us over the past few months together that we'll never be the same. May the scriptures continue to come to light through your diligent practices and the illumination of the Holy Spirit. May Jesus continue to lead and teach us to be his apprentices. And may we fulfill his commission as apprentices ourselves as we cooperatively participate with God's work in the lives of others.

By now, the consistency of the scriptures should be very clear. Everyone and everything emerges from within the same story – God's story. Every New Testament teaching about our new life in Jesus Christ overlaps and compliments the others. This is especially the case this week as we consider one of the New Testament's most contextualized metaphors for Jesus' followers:

"We are the temple of the living God."
(2 Corinthians 6:16)

To appreciate the significance of this verse (and others like it), let's trace this line of thought forward from its origin in Creation.

Creation. When God created, there was no temple. Creation was whole. There was no division between heavenly and earthly realms. Creation was God's resting place. It was home. God was fully present to people and people fully present to God. People walked with God in the garden. They talked with God. They knew the sound of God approaching. God wasn't present in special places; he was just present.

Israel. Part of the fallout of humanity's rebellion was the veil that came to exist between the heavenly and earthly realms of Creation. Humanity was exiled from the presence of God.

As we know, God did not stand idly by with his creative intentions for humanity shattered. In short order, redemption was underway. God called Abraham and set his descendants apart from the nations as cooperative participants in the redemptive plan for all creation.

Reimagining Discipleship

A major aspect of Israel's uniqueness was that they were called to build and care for the Temple – the one place on earth where the heavens and earth would remain intertwined...the place where God would dwell. The Temple was a testimony to the way things were supposed to be. It was filled with the imagery of creation as a reminder that God's rightful dwelling place with humanity was not confined to the Temple.

Unfortunately, Israel fell to the same fate as humanity: rebellion and sin. After repeated calls for Israel to repent and return to God and his purposes for the nation, the presence of God departed the Temple. Shortly thereafter, the building itself was destroyed in the Babylonian invasion. Rebellion once again led to exile: God's people were separated from their God-given dwelling place and from God's presence.

Jesus. With Jesus, everything changed. Sin was forgiven. Exile ended. God returned. He became present with his people in a manner anyone could see and experience, but no one could have predicted.

Everything the Temple represented and every religious purpose it served was fulfilled in and through Jesus Christ.

Then, despite all Jesus accomplished, his first disciples watched him ascend back into the heavens a short while after his resurrection. God departed again. And the disciples were told to wait... (Luke 24:49)

Church. On the day of Pentecost, the unthinkable happened. Per Jesus' instructions, his followers had gathered to wait and to pray. Then suddenly, in a scene reminiscent of 2 Chronicles 7 when the Spirit descended and filled Solomon's Temple:

> "There came a sound from heaven like a mighty rushing wind, and it filled the entire house where they were sitting. And divided tongues as of fire appeared to them and rested on each one of them. And they were all filled with the Holy Spirit..."
> (Acts 2:2-4a)

The Spirit of God returned as the people of Israel had long been hoping – only not in the manner they anticipated. It was not to a rebuilt Temple that the Spirit returned. No longer would a single high priest enter God's presence on one solitary day each year.

The Holy Spirit came and filled Jesus' disciples! In and through Jesus Christ, the disciples became the new Temple/s:

- the resting place of God

- the place in Creation that is once again whole – where God's presence resides

- the witness in the world of the way things are supposed to be and will one day be again fully

As Jesus' disciples, we are the temples of God in the world today. We are the intersection of the heavens and the earth. We are the witnesses of the way things were always supposed to be and the way they will one day be again. We are foretastes of what it truly means to be human. The Holy Spirit has come to dwell within us to empower us for this very high calling (Acts 1:8). In response, let us learn to live and walk by the Spirit:

- Living intentionally.
- Remembering where our story began & anticipating where it's going.
- Pursuing ongoing apprenticeship unto Jesus.
- Loving sacrificially.
- Living an eternal kind of life here & now.
- Establishing our allegiance in Jesus' eternal kingdom.
- Showing the rest of the world how to live well here & now...

WHEN JESUS IS KING.

Reimagining Discipleship

Day #1: In the context of God's story, describe the significance & meaning of being a temple of the Holy Spirit.

_____

_____

_____

_____

_____

Day #2: How does being a temple of the Holy Spirit influence your expectations as you look ahead in your pursuit of discipleship and God's purposes for your life?

_____

_____

_____

_____

_____

Day #3: What is the greatest thing that you'll take away from your _REIMAGINING DISCIPLESHIP_?

_____

_____

_____

How will you continue to cooperate with God's ongoing work in your life?

_____

_____

_____

_____

_____

DAILY PRACTICES: JESUS' WAY OF LIVING

Practice #7: "Celebrate" (Party!!)

You're almost there, but it's not over yet! One critical aspect of life for God's people is learning to remember and celebrate. So take some time tonight to plan a party – and party like you mean it! Not because the world likes to party, but because some things are worth celebrating... extravagantly! Celebrate together knowing that God commanded the Israelites throughout the Old Testament to remember what he had done and to celebrate it.

The details are up to you. Work it out together. Spend some money. Eat delicious food. Laugh. Tell stories. Stay up too late. Invest in a celebration worth remembering.

Ongoing Practices... This is just the beginning. By the grace of God, *REIMAGINING DISCIPLESHIP* has helped equip you with several options for ongoing discipleship. Now is your time to continue on. Grow. Learn. Become more and more like Jesus.

CLOSING PRAYER
Remembering.
Anticipating.
Participating.

TEMPLES: Notes & Reflections

_____
_____
_____
_____
_____
_____
_____
_____

EPILOGUE

We have reached the end of *REDISCOVERING DISCIPLESHIP* but find ourselves bonded together as Jesus' disciples. Regardless of where our paths take us from here, our lives are intertwined as we continue living in anticipation of our common future in Jesus' kingdom. The friendships we share are of an eternal quality. The sacrifices we make together and for each other are an eternal treasure and indicator of who and whose we are.

The future that awaits us is not an escape or a vacation – It's a kingdom. Let us live intentionally in the meantime. Not as a people "packing their bags" and waiting for departure. Let us live as cooperative participants in God's ongoing redemptive mission. Let us live as those who understand the narrative in which all humanity is taking its place...

WHEN JESUS IS KING.

As we conclude, it's difficult because there is so much more to say. There is so much more to do. There is so much more to celebrate...

By the grace of God, let us all continue on. Let us dive deeper into God's story. Let us learn it and submit ourselves into its narrative. Let us live to be about the King's business. Let us take our places in his eternal Kingdom. Let our lives take shape in discipleship unto Jesus Christ. And let us live to see God's good work multiplied in the lives of others – disciples making disciples, disciples laying down their lives in service of God and for the sake of his people everywhere. Let's be like Jesus and embrace his paradoxical invitation:

"If anyone would come after me, let him deny himself and take up his cross and follow me. For whoever would save his life will lose it, but whoever loses his life for my sake and the gospel's will save it."

—Jesus (Mark 8:34-35)

Appendix

OLD TESTAMENT READINGS

HISTORY:
Genesis
Exodus
Numbers 11-14, 16-17, 22-25
Deuteronomy 1-18, 28-34
Joshua
Judges
Ruth
1 & 2 Samuel
1 & 2 Kings
Ezra
Nehemiah
Esther

WISDOM:
Job
Psalms
Proverbs
Ecclesiastes

PROPHETS:
Isaiah 1-12, 37-66
Jeremiah 1-3, 20-31, 52
Ezekiel 10, 33-37
Daniel
Hosea
Jonah
Zephaniah
Haggai
Zechariah 7-14
Malachi

Leader's Guidelines

WHAT & HOW

The "What" & "How" for LIVING WELL WHEN JESUS IS KING are both very important. They are spelled out in the Series Preface at the beginning of each book.

As the leader, you should familiarize yourself with both "What" you're after and "How" you're going after it. The point of WJK isn't the weekly gatherings or the daily practices. The point is for people to learn to rethink and respond to Jesus Christ. The point is for us to live well before him here & now.

Keep in mind that such lives don't happen by accident. The "How" is very important. The scriptures are clear about the significance of learning to think differently and live in response to all that is underway in and through Jesus Christ. This is the clear model of Jesus with the disciples and also the Apostle Paul with his disciples. Our bodies and minds need to work together in submission to the process of discipleship – and then there's no limit to what God may do in and through us!

Along the way, sometimes people confuse the "How" (the stuff we're doing) with the "What". As the leader, it will be important to offset this tendency by reminding people why we're doing what we're doing. Again, the point isn't to "accomplish" the daily practices or attend gatherings. The point is for us to learn to live in cooperation with God's ongoing work in & around us. The point is to become a new kind of person. The point is to live well before Jesus Christ.

Finally, keep one eye fixed beyond the scope of the current study. The book should catalyze a process of transformation that, by the grace of God, will continue on for a lifetime. To equip people for a lifetime of discipleship and transformation (and to help prepare them as leaders themselves), it helps to be overly clear about what you're doing and why and how. So don't be afraid to repeat yourself...repeatedly.

May God bless and anoint you for the task that lies ahead. Thank you for putting yourself on the line for the sake of others. You'll do a great job! If you have questions or would like to talk something through regarding any of the Living Well When Jesus is King materials, feel free to email me: justlaugh911@gmail.com. I'd love to hear from you.

WEEKLY RHYTHM
- 3 days each week, read the upcoming week's article from the book. There will be 1-2 questions each day to contemplate & answer. Take notes on your answers to enrich the discussion once you're gathered.
- Daily Discipleship Practices
- Weekly Gathering:
  1. Prayer.
  2. Follow-up: what happened the previous week
  3. Read/review the current week's article and discuss people's answers to the Rethinking & Responding questions they've taken notes on over the course of the week.
  4. Connect with each other regarding whatever lies ahead in the coming week. Note how you can pray for and support each other. (Enjoy being part of each other's lives!)
  5. Closing Prayer.

GETTING STARTED

Prayerful Invitations
Prayerfully consider who God would have you invite to share in this journey. It's best in groups of 3-8 people. It can be equally effective for both new Christians and long-time saints. But it won't be for everyone. It takes time and commitment – be clear about this with those you invite. Be equally clear about what you're hoping to see as a result – genuine, sustainable transformation. REIMAGINING DISCIPLESHIP is a high stakes journey: it will cost you legitimate time and energy, but the reward is TREMENDOUS! As a leader, your enthusiasm and inspiration may make all the difference as people are deciding whether they'd like to join you. Make sure you help people "count the cost" accurately.

Initial Gathering

Have an initial gathering for those who show interest in joining the group. Talk through the preface materials in "First Things First." This includes a look at Luke 19, John 15 & Romans 12:1-2.

Discuss the EXPECTATIONS & COMMITMENT, but don't ask for a commitment during your initial gathering. Let people get back to you. Follow up with them sometime over the next week. Again, your enthusiasm and inspiration will make a big impact on those who have gathered.

You may want to decide/inform people of the time and place you'll be gathering should they commit to the group. You'll also need to leave enough time for those who commit to get a copy of the book between your initial gathering and Week #1.

PLANNING YOUR WEEKLY GATHERINGS

Plan on 60-90 minutes of good discussion time during your weekly gatherings. Be careful not to meet too long because the commitment needs to be sustainable for 16 weeks.

Here are some things for your group to consider:
- Where/when will you meet?
- Is the location child friendly? Should you arrange for group babysitting? How will you pay for it?
- Will you have dinner together? If so, how can you have dinner and still allow for at least 60 minutes of focused conversation?

ALONG THE WAY...
- Lead by example: Be on time. Be diligent in your daily practices. Be authentic & appropriate in sharing your experiences.
- Set aside time and energy to serve and encourage the other group members. Consider what you can do to facilitate God's work in each person in your group.
- Maintain regular communication. At least one contact (coffee/lunch, text, phone call, email, etc.) with each group member each week goes a long way toward group cohesion.

The Good News...in 100 Seconds

We've covered a lot of ground. One of the challenges we face if we take this all seriously is how to convey a fuller picture of the gospel for those God brings across our paths – especially when we have limited opportunity. The following is essentially what I arrived at on a recent trip to India during which I had the pleasure of visiting and preaching in several villages where our Christian brothers and sisters had been building relationships, preaching the gospel, and working to establish new local churches.

It's in my own words, of course, but I include it just to point out that **it is possible to convey the gospel in the context of God's story even in a very short period of time**. Anyway, I hope you enjoy it!

The world is broken.

It wasn't always. And it won't be forever.

The Creator God – the only true God – created everything. He created people to live with him and know him. To live in God's blessing and to govern creation on his behalf.

Unfortunately, people turned against the one true God and rebelled. They embraced sin and evil and worshiped other gods. And all creation felt the effects of their selfishness & rebellion: Disease. Hunger. Evil. Death.

But at just the right time, God's son stepped into creation. God became a man. He reminded people what it meant to be truly human. He loved. He healed. He set free those held captive.

The world responded by hanging him on a cross and killing him. Yet even as evil rose to its fullest power, it was defeated there on the cross. All sin was defeated. All evil. All rebellion.

Three days later, Jesus rose from the grave. Not a ghost. But no longer the same. In Jesus' resurrection, the renewal of all creation began. Jesus rose again – never again to know disease or sickness. Never again to experience pain. He rose again and he lives today!

After his resurrection, Jesus spent 40 days teaching and eating with his followers. And then he ascended into the heavens to await the time for his return. On that day, creation will once again be made whole. All the heavens and earth will dwell together. All will be renewed. And Jesus' faithful servants will join him in governing his kingdom.

We are here now as his followers to bring you this good news – that your sins can be forgiven if you will turn to Jesus. His kingdom stands open to you if you will turn to him and embrace him as your Lord and King and renounce all other gods.

This will not always be the case. There will come a day when Jesus returns in the fullness of his kingdom. All his people will rise to new life with him, and creation will be renewed according to God's good plan. But at that time will also come God's final judgment for those who refused Jesus' lordship in the time that they were given.

So we are here now in love and compassion to invite you to join us in turning to Jesus. Let us live TOGETHER in anticipation of the King's return and the restoration of all things. Let us give our lives to our King who first gave his life for us.

A Word from the Author

Justin lives in Castle Rock, Colorado, with his wife Jody and their three boys. Amidst their busy schedules, they are very thankful to share in the life of their community and their local church. And as often as possible, they also enjoy family adventures in the Rocky Mountains exploring, camping, hiking, and skiing.

Justin has been involved in many facets of church leadership, church planting, and missions since graduating from Greenville College in 1999. During that time, he has continued his education and training for ministry. He earned his Master's degree in Practical Theology at Regent University in 2008. And having recently completed his coursework at Fuller Theological Seminary, Justin now anticipates the completion of his Doctorate in Ministry in Missional Discipleship in the very near future.

To schedule speaking engagements or to discuss leadership training for LIVING WELL WHEN JESUS IS KING, please contact Justin at justlaugh911@gmail.com.

Thanks so much for investing yourself in this journey over the past several months. I pray that God has continued his good work in and around you as you have set this time apart for him, and that this is only the beginning!

I would love to hear stories of the work God has done and how REIMAGINING DISCIPLESHIP has impacted you and those around you. Please email your stories to justlaugh911@gmail.com. I can't wait to hear from you!

Justin

www.ingramcontent.com/pod-product-compliance
Lightning Source LLC
Chambersburg PA
CBHW071859020426
42331CB00010B/2581